TABLE OF CONTENTS

- A woman working full time, year-round earns **$10,800 less per year** than a man, based on median annual earnings. This disparity can add up to nearly a **half million dollars** over a career.

- On a percentage basis, a woman earns only **79 percent** of what a man earns. This is known as the "gender earnings ratio." The 21-percent difference between men's and women's earnings means that women are paid **less than $4 for every $5** paid to men.

- Although the gender pay gap has narrowed over time, at the current rate of change, **it will not close until 2059**, according to the Institute for Women's Policy Research.

- Lower career earnings result in an even greater disparity in retirement income. Median income for women ages 65 and older ($17,400) is **44 percent less** than the median income for men in the same age group ($31,200). Women 75 years and older are **almost twice as likely** as men to live in poverty.

- The gender pay gap varies widely across states, from a **low of 10 percent** in Washington, DC, to a **high of 35 percent** in Louisiana.

- Women's median earnings are **lower at every level of education**. In fact, women are often out-earned by men with less education: the typical woman with a graduate degree earns **$5,000 less** than the typical man with a bachelor's degree.

- Women of color face even larger gender pay gaps. Compared to white men, African-American women, on average, are paid **only 60 cents on the dollar** and Latinas are paid **only 55 cents on the dollar**.

- The pay gap typically grows with age. While women ages 18 to 24 earn **88 percent** of what their male counterparts earn, women over age 35 earn only **76 percent**.

- Economists believe that the gender pay gap is caused by complex factors. However, even when all those factors are taken into account, **as much as 40 percent** of the pay gap may be attributed to discrimination.

- American families depend on women's earnings. In the typical (median) household with a mother working outside the home, women contribute nearly **40 percent** of their family's total earnings.

- Women's increased participation in the paid labor force has been a major driver of economic growth in recent decades. According to the Council of Economic Advisers, the U.S. economy is **$2.0 trillion bigger today** than it would have been if women had not increased their participation and hours since 1970.

- Enacting policies that would narrow the gender pay gap and help more women work full time in the paid labor force would **decrease income inequality** and **lift many women out of poverty**.

GENDER PAY INEQUALITY
CONSEQUENCES FOR WOMEN, FAMILIES AND THE ECONOMY

INTRODUCTION

President John F. Kennedy signed the Equal Pay Act into law on June 10, 1963. The law mandates that men and women receive equal pay for "substantially equal" work at the same establishment.[1] A year later, Congress passed the Civil Rights Act of 1964. In addition to providing protections against discrimination based on an individual's national origin, race and religion, the Civil Rights Act prohibits discrimination on the basis of an individual's sex.[2]

Over the course of more than a half-century, these laws and more recent legislation have helped make it more likely that women receive equal pay for equal work. However, women still tend to be paid substantially less than men. Based on median annual earnings, a woman working full time, year-round typically earns only 79 cents for every dollar earned by her male counterpart.[3] The 21-percent difference in earnings (or 21 cents on the dollar) is known as the *"gender pay gap."*

The difference adds up—women's median earnings are $10,800 less per year than men's. Over the span of a career that yearly difference could accumulate to a half million dollars.[4]

The pay gap also dramatically affects what women receive in retirement because it reduces women's earnings. The major sources of retirement income, including Social Security and pension benefits, are largely calculated on the basis of career earnings. Income of women ages 65 and older ($17,400) is 44 percent less than the median income for men in the same age group ($31,200). As a result of this and other factors, a higher percentage of women than men end up living in poverty after age 65.

The gap between men's and women's median earnings has decreased substantially since the 1960s and 1970s, when women first began entering the labor force in large numbers. However, at the current rate of change, the gender pay gap will not close until 2059.[5]

Young women today may not be aware of the extent of the gender pay gap because they typically begin their careers facing a relatively small pay gap. Women ages 18 to 24 earn approximately 88 percent of what their male counterparts earn. However, for most women the gender pay gap grows as they continue in their careers and start families. Today, women ages 45 to 54 typically earn only 70 percent of what their male counterparts earn.

Some women have little choice but to stay out of the workforce for a period of time after they have children because quality child care is unavailable or prohibitively expensive.[6] When, and if, they return to work, many women are confronted with a "mommy penalty"—earning less than women who are not mothers. Fathers, on the other hand, often benefit from a "daddy bonus," and earn more than men who are not fathers.[7]

Other factors also help explain the gender pay gap. Occupational segregation and steering can lead women to study and work in lower-paying fields and to have lower-paying jobs within many fields. In addition, some economists have found that as much as 40 percent of the gender pay gap could be due to factors that cannot be measured, including outright gender discrimination.[8]

The disparity between men's and women's earnings is not inevitable. As this report makes clear, there are several steps the United States can take to help shrink the gender pay gap. Following the example of many other industrialized countries, the United States could adopt family-friendly workplace policies such as paid family and sick leave, universal child care and flexible workplace arrangements. This would make it easier for both men and women to balance the demands of work and home, while ensuring that women are not penalized for becoming mothers and caring for their families. In addition, passing the Equal Rights Amendment to guarantee equal rights under the Constitution for women, and passing the Paycheck Fairness Act to build on prior legislation would help ensure that women receive equal pay for equal work.

THE GENDER PAY GAP

How Economists Calculate the Gender Pay Gap

Women contribute significantly to the U.S. economy, and their contributions have increased markedly over the last half-century. In 1963, only 44 percent of prime working-age women (ages 25 to 54) were in the labor force. Around that time, women held fewer than one in three jobs. Today, about 75 percent of prime working-age women are in the labor force and women hold almost half (49 percent) of all jobs.[9]

Despite these vast changes, women's earnings typically still lag significantly behind men's. In 2014 (the latest year for which data are available), men's median annual earnings were roughly $50,400 while women's median annual earnings were only $39,600—a difference of $10,800.[10] The ratio of women's to men's median earnings—known as the *"gender earnings ratio"*—was approximately 79 percent. That leaves a difference in earnings of 21 percent (or 21 cents on the dollar) which is commonly referred to as the *"gender pay gap."* It means that the typical woman still earns less than $4 for every $5 earned by the typical man.

The 79-percent gender earnings ratio is a significant improvement from 1963, when women's median earnings were just 59 percent of men's (see **Figure 1**).[11] Unfortunately, much of the progress in recent decades has been due to the decline in men's earnings.[12] Men's real (inflation-adjusted) annual earnings most recently peaked in 2000 and are now 5 percent lower than in 1973.[13]

The disparity between men's and women's income adds up over time. According to the National Women's Law Center, for the typical woman working full time, year-round, the annual gap would grow to more than $430,000 over a 40-year period.[14] Using a different methodology, the Institute for

Women's Policy Research (IWPR) has estimated that the typical woman born between 1955 and 1959 who worked full time, year-round each year lost more than $530,000 by the time she reached age 59.[15]

For many women, the lifetime earnings gap is significantly larger. Women of color, who face larger pay gaps when compared to white men, and college-educated women, stand to lose even more over their careers. The typical African-American woman would earn more than $877,000 less than the typical white man over 40 years, and the typical Latina would earn roughly $1,007,000 less.[16] Women with higher levels of education also face larger pay gaps than the typical woman. IWPR has estimated that the typical college-educated woman born between 1955 and 1959 lost more than $797,000 by age 59.[17]

Figure 1: Median Annual Earnings
Women and men working full time, year-round, 1960 to 2014

Source: Income and Poverty in the United States, U.S. Census Bureau
Note: Annual real median earnings, rounded to the nearest hundred dollars

Career-Long Wage Disparities Jeopardize Women's Retirement Security

The wage disparities women experience during their careers dramatically lower their incomes in retirement. This is largely because the most common sources of income in retirement are often based on an individual's work and earnings history. Those sources include Social Security benefits, pensions, earnings and personal savings.[18] In 2014, the median annual income of women ages 65 and older was $17,400, only 56 percent of men's the same age.[19] In other words, women face an income gap of 44 percent in retirement, a difference that is more than twice the overall gender pay gap.

While men 65 years and older collectively received nearly $965 million in income in 2014, women in that age group received roughly $641 million—$324 million less than men (see **Figure 2**).[20] That is despite the fact that women outnumber men in that age group.[21]

Interestingly, women's collective income from Social Security ($276.8 million) was only slightly less than men's. But Social Security income accounted for 43 percent of women's total income, compared with 30 percent of men's total income.

Earnings are playing an increasingly important role in the financial security of older women. The share of women over the age of 65 in the labor force has been increasing over the past two decades, rising from less than 9 percent in early 1995 to more than 15 percent today.[22] In 2014, women 65 years and older collectively received $148.9 million in earnings, accounting for roughly 23 percent of their total income.[23] Women today are more likely than men to postpone retirement, according to a recent survey by the National Institute on Retirement Security. While 31 percent of men delayed or planned to delayed

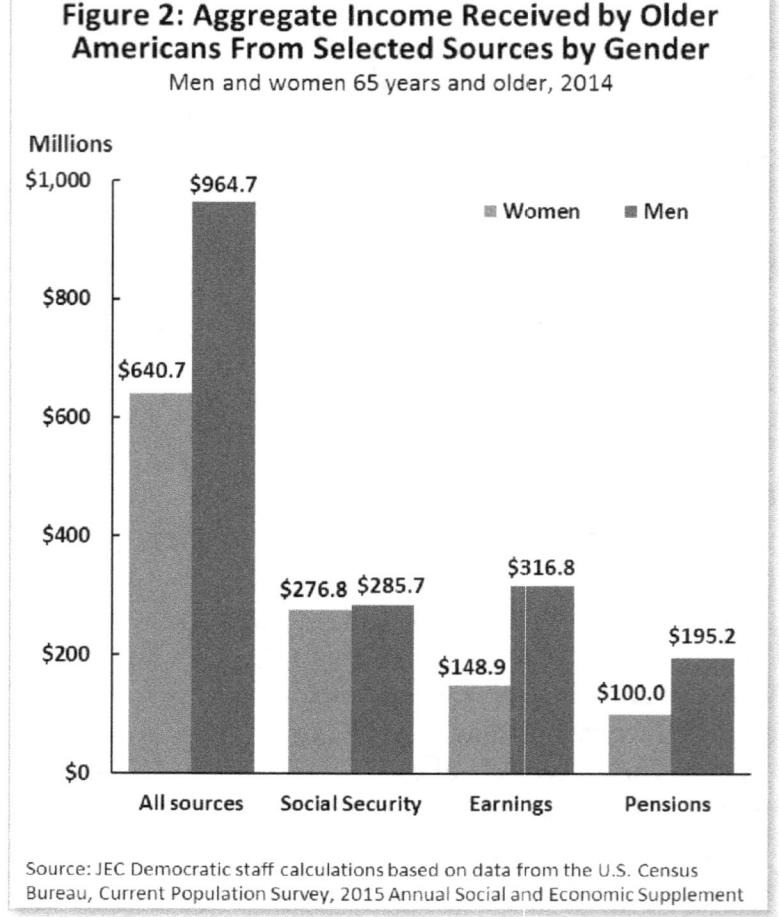

Figure 2: Aggregate Income Received by Older Americans From Selected Sources by Gender
Men and women 65 years and older, 2014

Source: JEC Democratic staff calculations based on data from the U.S. Census Bureau, Current Population Survey, 2015 Annual Social and Economic Supplement

retirement, 41 percent of women did or planned to. The women surveyed reported a number of reasons for needing to delay retirement, including to make up for lower earnings during their career and for time spent out of the labor force to care for children and other family members.[24]

The Gender Pay Gap Affects What Women Receive From Social Security

In the United States, retirement security is often described as a three-legged stool, supported by Social Security benefits, pension income and private savings. For women, the stool rests most heavily on the Social Security leg. This is because women are less likely than men to have pension income and personal savings. In fact, for nearly one in five older women, Social Security benefits are their only source of income.[25] And for many, Social Security benefits are their only source of income that is both guaranteed for life and whose value is protected against inflation.[26]

Despite the relative importance of Social Security for older women, their benefits are typically smaller than men's. Social Security benefits are calculated based on an individual's earnings history, but women generally have lower pay during their working years and spend fewer years in the paid labor force than men. As a result, the average monthly Social Security benefit for female retirees is 79 percent of what it is for male retirees.[27]

Women Receive Less Pension Income Than Men

Women are less likely than men to receive income from traditional pension plans.[28] Some are ineligible to participate in employer-sponsored retirement plans because they do not meet the minimum criteria for eligibility. This may be the result of time spent out of the workforce caring for children and other family members. Women are also more likely to work in jobs that do not offer retirement plans.[29] Among those women who have pension income, their income tends to be smaller than men's. This is due to the fact that payments from these retirement plans are typically calculated based on a worker's tenure and salary during peak-earnings years. Women's median income from company or union pensions is 53 percent of men's median income from those same sources. Women also receive smaller distributions from federal, state and local government pension plans.[30]

A Higher Percentage of Women Live in Poverty After Age 65

At every age, women are more likely than men to live in poverty. But the disparity is greatest for older women. Not only do they typically have lower earnings than men, they also are more likely to live longer and have higher medical expenses than men.[31] As a result, women are more likely than men to outlive their retirement savings. Women are 1.6 times as likely as men to live in poverty once they reach age 65, and nearly twice as likely to live in poverty once they reach age 75 (see **Figure 3**).[32]

Today, more than 12 percent of women ages 65 and older and nearly 15 percent of women ages 75 and older live below the poverty line. Without Social Security benefits, the number of women ages 65 and older in poverty would be even higher, increasing from 3.1 million to roughly 11.7 million and pushing their poverty rate from 12.1 percent to 45.6 percent.[33]

Poverty rates are especially striking among women who live alone. Among women ages 65 and older living alone, nearly 20 percent are in poverty. In comparison, just over 12 percent of men ages 65 and older living alone are in poverty. Women of color also have very high rates of poverty after age 65. African-American and Hispanic women are the most likely to live in poverty in old age as a result of their

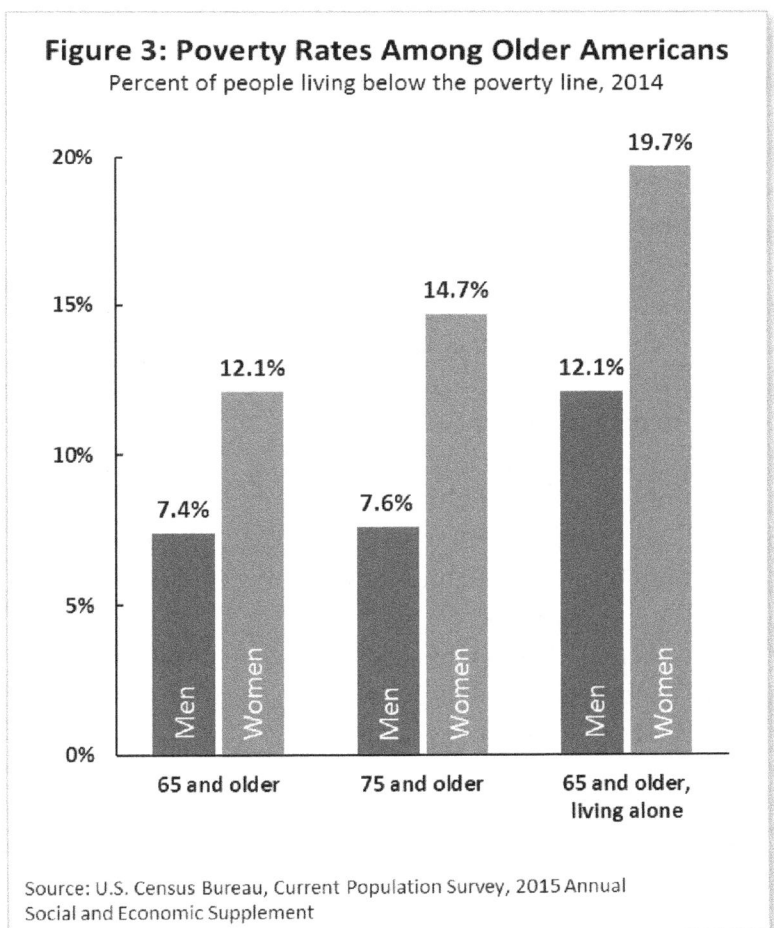

Figure 3: Poverty Rates Among Older Americans
Percent of people living below the poverty line, 2014

Source: U.S. Census Bureau, Current Population Survey, 2015 Annual Social and Economic Supplement

lower career earnings. One in five women of color ages 65 and older are poor. That share jumps to one in three for women of color ages 65 and older who live alone.[34]

DISPARITIES BY RACE, AGE AND REGION

Many Women of Color Face Larger Gender Pay Gaps When Compared to White Men

Women of all races and ethnicities face a pay gap when compared with men of the same race or ethnicity. However, women of color suffer both because of their gender and their race.[35]

In 2014, the median earnings of white women were $41,800, or 75 percent of white men's.[36] Women of color fared better compared to men of their same race: African-American women's earnings were 82 percent of African-American men's, Asian women's earnings were 81 percent of Asian men's, and Hispanic women's earnings were 88 percent of Hispanic men's.[37]

However, women of color earn even less when compared to white men, the largest demographic segment of the workforce (see **Figure 4**).[38] African-American women earn only 60 percent of what white men earn, and Hispanic women only 55 percent of what white men earn. Asian women face the smallest gap relative to white men, earning 84 percent of white men's earnings.

Women of color are under-represented in high-paying STEM fields. This contributes to the larger pay gaps many women of color experience relative to white men. African-American women make up roughly 6 percent of the workforce, yet they account for just 2 percent of workers in STEM fields. Likewise, Hispanic women make up 7 percent of the workforce, but they account for less than 2 percent of STEM workers.[39] Asian women, on the other hand, make up a larger share of the STEM workforce (4 percent), when compared to their share of the workforce across all occupations (3 percent).[40]

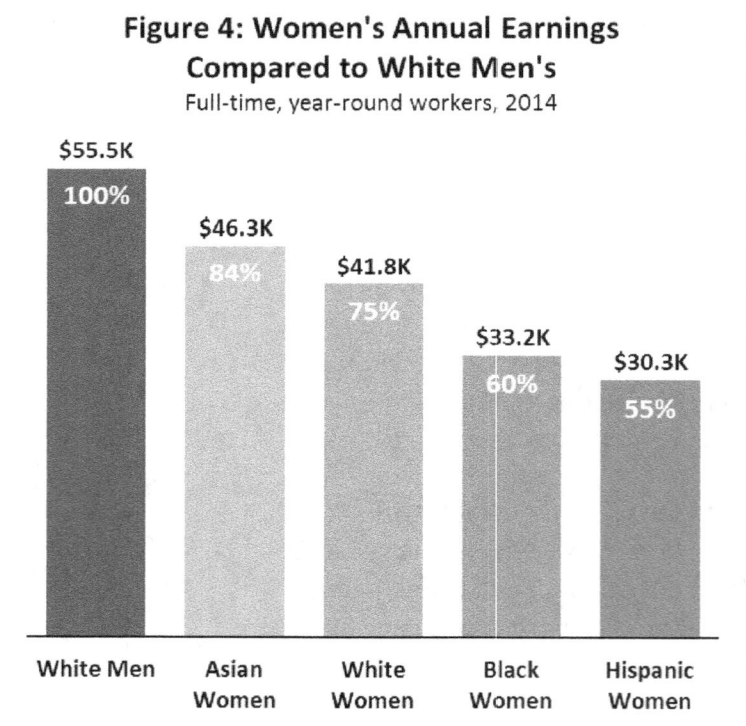

Figure 4: Women's Annual Earnings Compared to White Men's
Full-time, year-round workers, 2014

- White Men — $55.5K — 100%
- Asian Women — $46.3K — 84%
- White Women — $41.8K — 75%
- Black Women — $33.2K — 60%
- Hispanic Women — $30.3K — 55%

Source: JEC Democratic staff calculations based on data from the U.S. Census Bureau

Notes: "White" refers to "White Alone, not Hispanic"; "Black" refers to "Black Alone or in Combination"; "Hispanic" refers to "Hispanic (any race)"; "Asian" refers to "Asian Alone"; dollars are rounded to nearest hundred; full-time, year-round workers include those who work 50 to 52 weeks on a full-time basis

Hispanic and African-American women face additional challenges in the labor force. They are more likely than white women to hold jobs that offer fewer hours and more likely to work part time involuntarily.[41] Hispanic and African-American women also are less likely to have access to benefits such as paid sick leave, paid family leave and flexible work schedules.[42]

The Disparity Between Male and Female Earnings Increases With Age

Women today begin their careers earning almost as much as their male colleagues. Those between the ages of 18 and 24 earn approximately 88 percent of what their male counterparts earn. Women between the ages of 25 and 34 earn slightly less—approximately 86 percent of what their male counterparts earn (see **Figure 5**).[43] However, after age 35, women's earnings typically grow more slowly than men's, resulting in a larger pay gap for older women.[44] Among workers 35 and older, women's median earnings in 2014 were 76 percent of men's.[45]

Young women today may not be fully aware of the extent of the gender pay gap. Not only do they earn almost as much as their male colleagues, they have also spent less time in the workforce and are less likely to have experienced discrimination on the job. Among all women, less than one in five (18 percent) say they have experienced gender discrimination in the workplace, according to a Pew Research Center survey. However, only 15 percent of millennial women reported that they had been the victim of gender discrimination at work, compared with 23 percent of baby boomer women.[46]

Economists attribute the larger gender pay gap faced by older women in part to the fact that women in the paid workforce effectively are penalized for having children. Mothers of young children are less likely to be in the labor force than similarly aged women without children.[47] Stepping out of the labor force to raise children can negatively affect a woman's work experience and tenure and may result in forgoing merit and other wage increases. This can substantially lower a woman's lifetime earnings.[48]

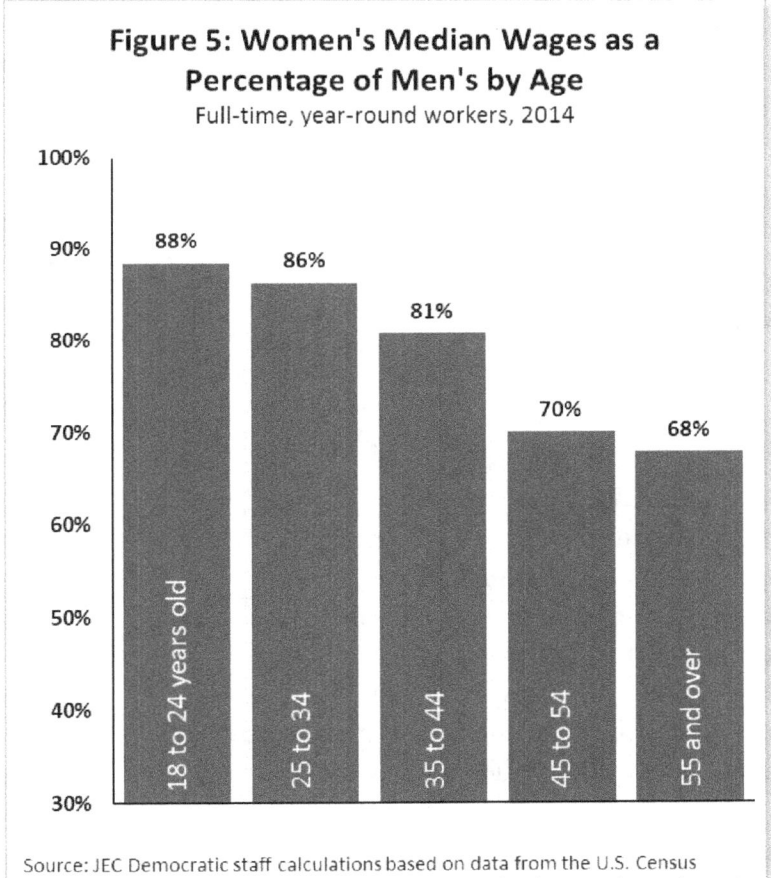

Figure 5: Women's Median Wages as a Percentage of Men's by Age
Full-time, year-round workers, 2014

- 18 to 24 years old: 88%
- 25 to 34: 86%
- 35 to 44: 81%
- 45 to 54: 70%
- 55 and over: 68%

Source: JEC Democratic staff calculations based on data from the U.S. Census Bureau, Current Population Survey, 2015 Annual Social and Economic Supplement

Working mothers may also suffer because of a perception by some employers that women with children are generally less committed to their work.[49] A woman can face discrimination even if her employer believes that she *might* become pregnant.[50]

Many women now wait to start families until they have established their careers. In 1970, the average age of first-time mothers was just over 21 years. By 2014, it had risen to over 26 years.[51] This has helped increase the earnings of more young women relative to their male counterparts, and delay the increase in the gender pay gap that occurs as women get older.

Between 1989 and today, the gender pay gap for women ages 25 to 34 decreased from 21 to 14 percent. Over the same period, the gender pay gap for women ages 35 to 44 narrowed from 37 to 19 percent. However, the gap for young women (ages 18 to 24) has remained steady at about 12 percent.[52]

The Size of the Gender Pay Gap Varies Widely in Different Parts of the Country

Women have not yet reached pay parity in any of the 50 states or the District of Columbia (see **Table 1**). In 21 states, the ratio between women's and men's median earnings is less than the national gender earnings ratio of 78.6 percent. For example, in Louisiana, women's median earnings are less than two-thirds (65 percent) of men's, the worst ratio in any state. Women fare only slightly better in Utah and Wyoming, where they typically earn only 68 percent and 69 percent, respectively, of what their male counterparts earn.[53]

On the other hand, in 29 states and the District of Columbia the ratio between women's and men's median earnings is higher than the national ratio. The gender earnings ratio is highest in the

Table 1: Gender Pay Gap by State, 2014 *Ordered largest to smallest*			
Rank	**State**	**Gender Pay Gap**	**Gender Earnings Ratio**
51	Louisiana	34.7%	65.3%
50	Utah	32.4%	67.6%
49	Wyoming	31.2%	68.8%
48	West Virginia	30.0%	70.0%
47	North Dakota	28.7%	71.3%
46	Alabama	27.4%	72.6%
45	Idaho	27.2%	72.8%
44	Oklahoma	26.5%	73.5%
43	Montana	25.8%	74.2%
42	Michigan	25.5%	74.5%
41	Indiana	24.8%	75.2%
40	New Hampshire	24.3%	75.7%
39	South Dakota	23.8%	76.2%
38	Mississippi	23.0%	77.0%
37	Kansas	23.0%	77.0%
36	Washington	23.0%	77.0%
35	Iowa	22.7%	77.3%
34	Missouri	22.6%	77.4%
33	Ohio	22.2%	77.8%
32	New Mexico	21.9%	78.1%
31	Arkansas	21.8%	78.2%
30	Texas	21.2%	78.8%
29	Maine	21.2%	78.8%
28	Nebraska	21.1%	78.9%
27	Wisconsin	21.1%	78.9%
26	Illinois	20.9%	79.1%
25	Pennsylvania	20.8%	79.2%
24	Kentucky	20.1%	79.9%
23	Virginia	19.8%	80.2%
22	South Carolina	19.8%	80.2%
21	New Jersey	19.7%	80.3%
20	Alaska	19.2%	80.8%
19	Delaware	19.0%	81.0%
18	Tennessee	18.5%	81.5%
17	Minnesota	18.4%	81.6%
16	Rhode Island	18.3%	81.7%
15	Georgia	18.2%	81.8%
14	Colorado	18.1%	81.9%
13	Massachusetts	18.0%	82.0%
12	Oregon	17.8%	82.2%
11	Connecticut	17.4%	82.6%
10	Vermont	16.2%	83.8%
9	Arizona	15.9%	84.1%
8	California	15.8%	84.2%
7	North Carolina	15.3%	84.7%
6	Florida	15.1%	84.9%
5	Nevada	14.9%	85.1%
4	Maryland	14.6%	85.4%
3	Hawaii	14.1%	85.9%
2	New York	13.2%	86.8%
1	District of Columbia	10.4%	89.6%
	Puerto Rico	-4.6%	104.6%

The vertical arrow on the left of the table ranges from "Worse" (top) to "Better" (bottom).

Source: JEC Democratic staff calculations based on data from the U.S. Census Bureau, 2014 American Community Survey (1-year estimates)
Notes: Data are based on median annual earnings of those who have worked full time, year-round in the past 12 months; earnings data are in 2014 inflation-adjusted dollars, rounded to nearest hundred dollars; population 16 years and over with earnings

District of Columbia, where women bring home roughly 90 cents for every dollar earned by men. New York, Hawaii, Maryland and Nevada also rank highly, with women's median earnings at least 85 percent of men's.

Across the country, most states have implemented laws to protect against gender discrimination.[54] All but three states prohibit gender discrimination by employers. More than two-thirds of states have added additional protections to prohibit retaliation or discrimination against workers who are involved in investigations related to unequal pay practices. And half of states have laws to limit the reasons employers can use for justifying unequal pay practices.

There appears to be a correlation between strong equal pay laws and smaller gender pay gaps. The states with the strongest equal pay laws tend to have smaller gender pay gaps, including California (16 percent), Vermont (16 percent), Tennessee (18 percent), Minnesota (18 percent) and Illinois (21 percent). The states with no legal protections tend to have larger gender pay gaps, including Alabama (27 percent) and Mississippi (23 percent). However, although South Carolina (20 percent) does not have an equal pay law on the books, it has a smaller gender pay gap than many states with protections. Still, robust protections against gender pay discrimination by themselves do not close the gender pay gap. For example, North Dakota has also implemented several protections but has a gender pay gap of roughly 29 percent.

THE BROADER COSTS OF GENDER PAY INEQUALITY

America's Families Depend on Women's Earnings

When both the Equal Pay Act and Civil Rights Act were enacted, women played a far smaller role in the workforce than they do today.[55] Fewer than half of prime-age women (ages 25 to 54) were in the labor force.[56] About two-thirds of married women stayed home.[57]

The women's equality movement sparked vast changes in women's roles. Widespread access to household technologies such as electric washing machines, dryers and dishwashers helped to free up time for women to take jobs in the paid workforce. More reliable contraception enabled women to delay starting families while they pursued careers.[58]

Today, nearly three-quarters of all prime-age women are in the workforce (either holding or seeking a job). More than 55 percent of married women work outside the home and almost 40 percent of them are their family's primary wage earner.[59] More than two-thirds of mothers with children under the age of 18 are in the labor force.[60]

Today, more than six out of every 10 households with children have no stay-at-home parent. This includes families headed by married couples with two working parents and families headed by a single working parent. By comparison, only four out of 10 households had no stay-at-home parent in 1965.[61] Currently more than 47 million children live in a household with no stay-at-home parent.[62]

Middle-class families have increasingly come to rely on women's incomes to make ends meet. In the typical (median) household with a mother working outside the home, women contribute nearly 40 percent of their family's total earnings.[63] And of families with a mother working outside the home, 34 percent depend solely on the mother's wages (see **Figure 6**).

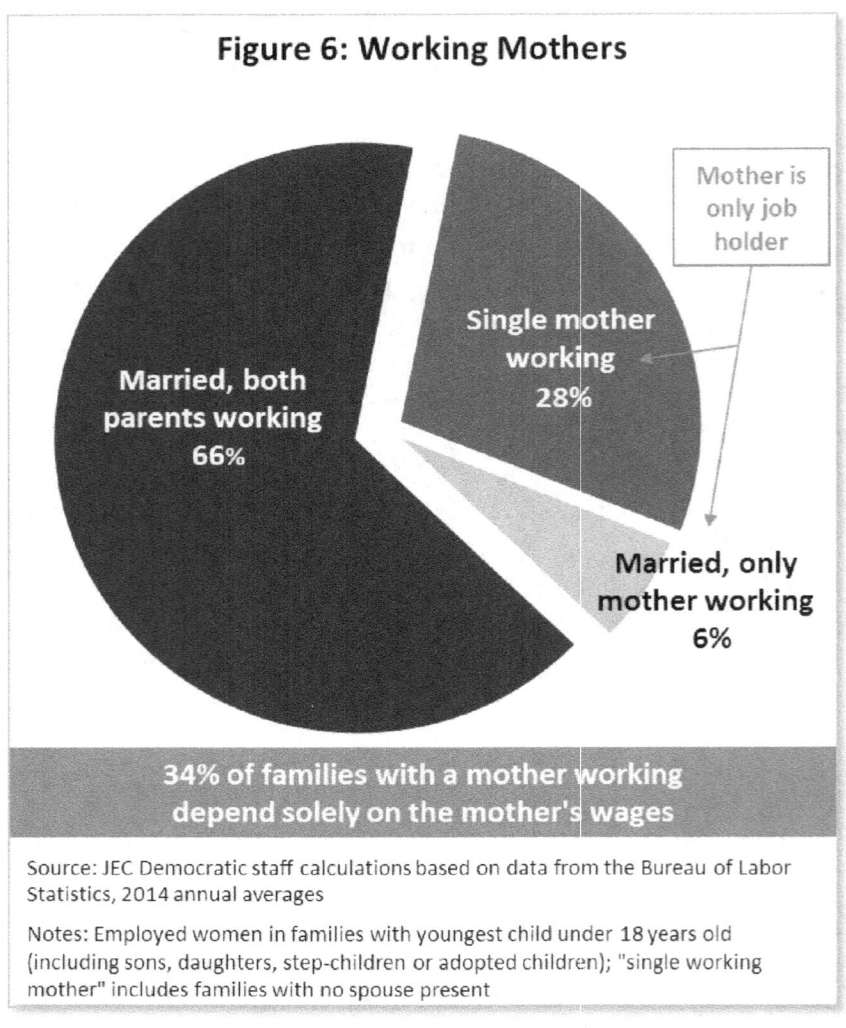

Figure 6: Working Mothers

Married, both parents working 66%

Single mother working 28%

Mother is only job holder

Married, only mother working 6%

34% of families with a mother working depend solely on the mother's wages

Source: JEC Democratic staff calculations based on data from the Bureau of Labor Statistics, 2014 annual averages

Notes: Employed women in families with youngest child under 18 years old (including sons, daughters, step-children or adopted children); "single working mother" includes families with no spouse present

Low-income families are even more dependent upon women's earnings. The vast majority of these families are supported solely by a mother, and often by a single mother.[64] Mothers in families in the bottom 20 percent of the earnings distribution typically contribute 89 percent of their family's earnings (see **Figure 7**). More than one-quarter of families headed by single mothers are poor. Closing the pay gap would cut the poverty rate for these families almost in half, from 28.7 percent to 15.0 percent.[65]

Women's earnings are crucial for many families because of increased pressures stemming from the growing costs of raising children. Between 1960 and 2013, the amount a typical middle-income, two-parent family spent to care for a child through the age of 17 increased 24 percent in real (inflation-adjusted) terms.[66] The composition of these expenses has also changed, with the share of spending going to child care and education growing roughly ninefold from just 2 percent in 1960 to 18 percent in 2013.[67] The share of family income spent on health care doubled to 8 percent during that time.[68]

Closing the gender pay gap and enabling women to maximize their earning potential would substantially improve the financial position of America's families, helping them better afford quality child care, housing, health care and education.

Gender Pay Inequality Hurts the Economy

Increasing pay equity and women's participation in the labor force is more than a personal or family issue. It is also necessary for a robust economy. The size of a country's labor force is a key determinant of its potential economic growth. And according to the Federal Reserve, "The most important driver of the rise in aggregate labor force participation [in the United States] over the past 30 years was the dramatic increase in labor force participation of prime-age women, including married women and women with children."[69] In fact, the U.S. economy is $2.0 trillion bigger today than it would have been if women had not increased their participation and hours in the labor force, according to a recent estimate by the Council of Economic Advisers.[70]

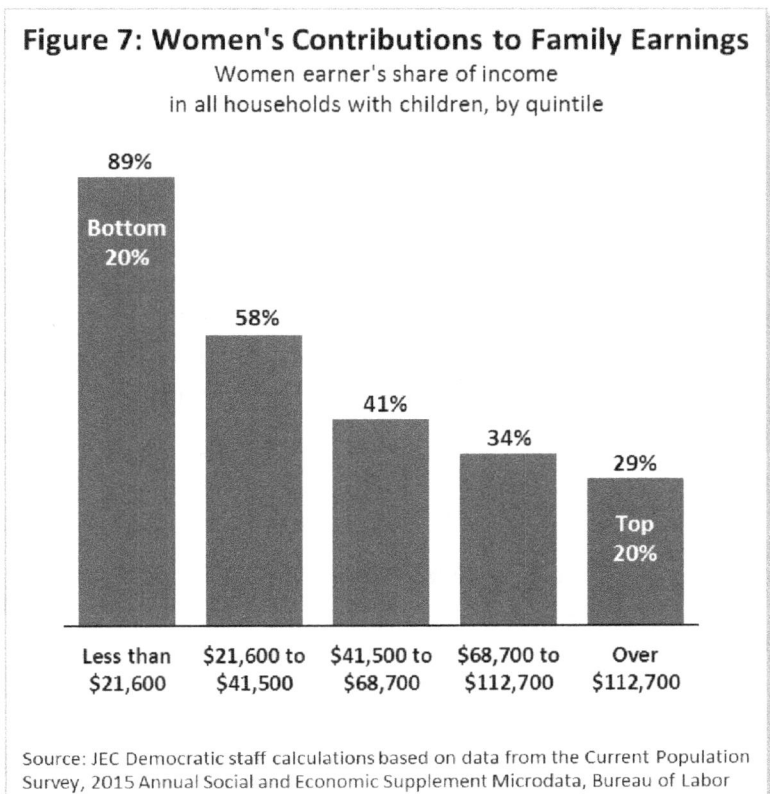

Figure 7: Women's Contributions to Family Earnings
Women earner's share of income in all households with children, by quintile

Source: JEC Democratic staff calculations based on data from the Current Population Survey, 2015 Annual Social and Economic Supplement Microdata, Bureau of Labor Statistics

Notes: Based on 2014 annual earnings; children are defined as those under 18 years old; includes households with and without a partner; income ranges are rounded to nearest hundred dollars

The United States was once a global leader in women's labor force participation. However, the United States has lost ground due in part to the absence of family-friendly policies in the workplace.[71] Its ranking fell from seventh out of 24 countries in the Organisation for Economic Co-operation and Development (OECD) in 1990 for labor force participation among prime-working age women, to 14th out of 34 countries in 2014.[72]

In an efficient economy, workers are employed in the jobs best suited for their skills. But this is not the case for all workers today. Many women face barriers in the workplace that prevent them from utilizing their skills and achieving their full economic potential. Discrimination is one such barrier, but occupational segregation and outdated workplace policies also play a role. Eliminating these barriers would benefit women, their families and the economy. International Monetary Fund President Christine Lagarde has cautioned, "By not fully engaging half of the population, we all lose out."[73]

The Institute for Women's Policy Research has estimated that the earnings of roughly 60 percent of women would increase if women were "paid the same as men of the same age with similar education and hours of work." Overall, IWPR estimates that closing the gender pay gap would give an additional $447.6 billion to women and their families, and would cut their poverty rate in half.[74]

Boosting women's earnings would increase spending by households, generating additional consumer demand. Stimulating demand increases production and leads to economic growth. According to the OECD, the U.S. economy would be 5 percent larger in 2030 if the gap between men's and women's labor force participation were cut in half.[75] Having more women working full time in the paid labor force also could decrease income inequality and lift many women out of poverty, which would reduce government spending on programs such as Medicaid and the Supplemental Nutrition Assistance Program (SNAP).[76]

FACTORS THAT CONTRIBUTE TO THE GENDER PAY GAP

The causes of the gender pay gap are complex. One of the most startling factors is that a lack of family-friendly workplace policies in the United States essentially means that millions of American women are penalized for becoming mothers and caring for their children. Although some larger American corporations have instituted such policies in order to retain highly educated and skilled employees, most companies do not offer policies that would make it easier for women or men to step out of the workforce or reduce their hours to care for their children while enabling them to return to full-time work without compromising their earning potential. This dynamic is a major contributor to the gender pay gap.

Differences in fields of study and employment also often lead to substantial differences in pay. This is partly the result of personal choice, but it is also strongly influenced by slow-to-change societal norms and steering of women into lower-paying, female-dominated occupations.

Research has shown that even when these and other factors are taken into consideration, there remains a gap between what men and women typically earn. It is thought that this is due to persistent discrimination against women in the workplace.

Women Are More Likely Than Men to Interrupt Their Careers to Care for Children

Women are significantly more likely than men to leave a job or reduce their hours to care for children.[77] This makes them more likely to miss out on scheduled or merit pay increases, and it negatively affects their tenure and on-the-job experience. According to one study, 10 years after graduating from college, 23 percent of mothers were out of the workforce and 17 percent were employed part time. In contrast, 1 percent of fathers were out of the workforce, and only 2 percent were employed part time.[78]

Among parents of young children, mothers are less likely to be employed than fathers. About 56 percent of mothers with children under the age of three work outside the home, compared with nearly 90 percent of fathers with young children.[79] More than half (59 percent) of first-time mothers who worked during their pregnancy were working three months after giving birth, and about one in five (21 percent) were not working after 12 months.[80]

It is common for working parents to face conflicts when they try to balance the demands of work and family, but the burden of meeting family responsibilities often falls to mothers. 39 percent of mothers report having taken a significant amount of time off to care for a child or family member, and 27 percent report having quit their job (see **Figure 8**).

By contrast, only about one in four fathers (24 percent) report that they took a significant amount of time off and just 10 percent quit their job because of family responsibilities, according to a Pew Research Center survey of working parents.[81] Not surprisingly, mothers are twice as likely as fathers to report that having children has made it more difficult to advance their career or job.[82]

A shortage of affordable quality child care and the lack of paid family leave force many women to leave the labor force for a period of time to raise children. This affects families across income levels. However, it particularly affects lower-income households who are more likely to have a stay-at-home mother than higher-income households.[83]

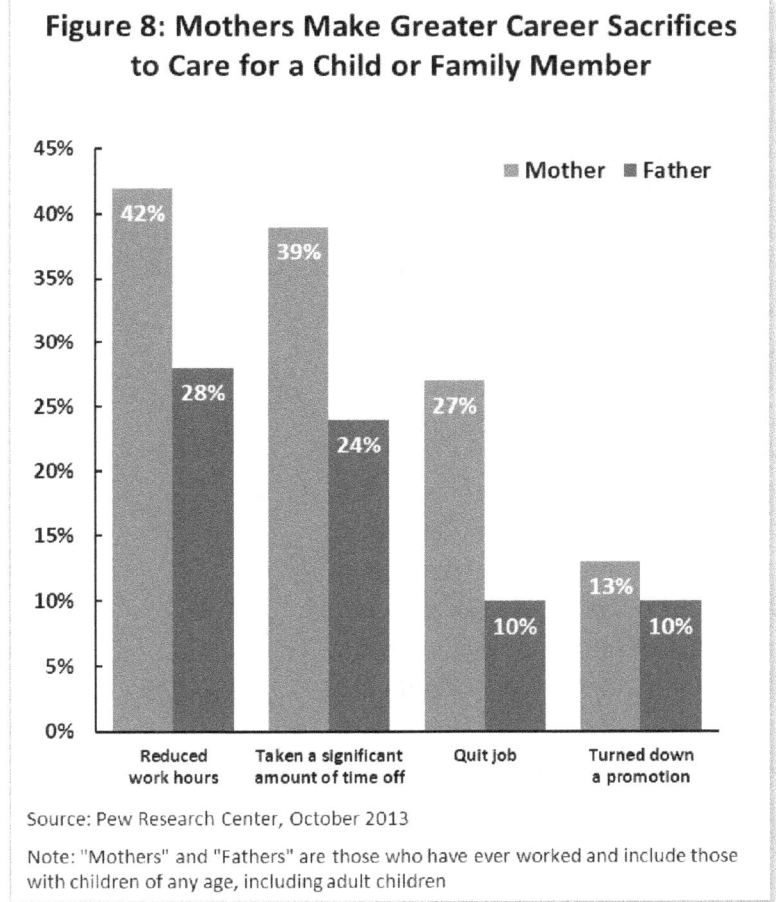

Figure 8: Mothers Make Greater Career Sacrifices to Care for a Child or Family Member

Source: Pew Research Center, October 2013

Note: "Mothers" and "Fathers" are those who have ever worked and include those with children of any age, including adult children

Stepping out of the labor force, even temporarily, has a significant impact on a woman's career and her earning potential. For example, if a mother who earns an annual salary of $40,000 decides to stay home with her two children for five years, she would lose more than the $200,000 cumulative salary she would have earned had she continued to work. She would also miss out on annual cost-of-living adjustments, raises, and contributions to Social Security and her retirement account. On the other hand, a father working the same job who does not take time away would continue to receive raises, cost-of-living adustments and other benefits, in addition to his salary.

Research shows that mothers with access to paid maternity leave are significantly more likely to return to their employer and to maintain their pre-leave wages. They are better able to build tenure and experience in their jobs and to remain in positions that are well-suited to their interests and education. Consequently, ensuring that women have access to paid maternity leave can help to raise mothers' earnings and close the pay gap.[84] Moreover, there are well-documented child and maternal health benefits as a result of the uninterrupted bonding time that paid parental leave makes possible.[85]

Working Mothers Often Pay a "Mommy Penalty"

Career interruptions can hurt a mother's earnings. Data suggest that women suffer a "mommy penalty" after they have children, earning 3 percent less than women who do not have children. The opposite is true for fathers, who earn on average 15 percent more than men without children (see **Figure 9**).[86]

Some of this disparity may result from differences in occupations and hours between men and women who have children and those who do not. For example, women may reduce their hours or take time off after the birth or adoption of a child, while fathers may increase their hours. The resulting gaps in experience and pay often persist long after a mother has returned to working full time.

However, studies suggest that fathers may also be rewarded beyond what differences in occupation or experience would justify. Some employers may believe that women are more likely than men to interrupt their careers to care for children and perceive motherhood as a signal of lower levels of commitment and professional competence. On the other hand, employers may view fatherhood as a signal of increased work commitment and stability.[87]

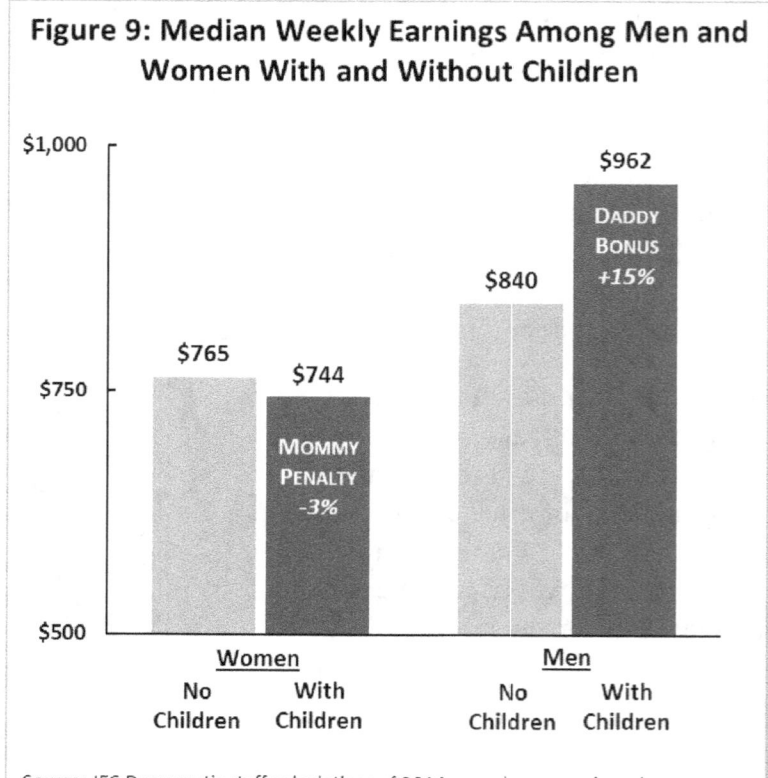

Figure 9: Median Weekly Earnings Among Men and Women With and Without Children

Source: JEC Democratic staff calculations of 2014 annual averages based on monthly data from the Current Population Survey, Bureau of Labor Statistics

Notes: Men and women ages 25 to 54 years old who are full-time paid employees; mothers and fathers include those with children living within the household who are under 18 years old; rounded to nearest percentage point

Women Are More Likely Than Men to be Primary Caregivers of Other Family Members

Mothers are significantly more likely than fathers to take time off to care for a sick child, elderly parent or other relative.[88] This is partly a financial decision because women tend to have the lower earnings in their household—60 percent of married working women earn less than their husband. Although men and women report having access to family-friendly workplace policies in roughly the same percentages, surveys suggest men are significantly less likely to use their leave because they believe that they would be viewed negatively by management and coworkers for taking time off.[89] Women may also choose to cut back their hours in order to balance family responsiblities and work instead of using leave.[90]

Today, many women carry the added responsibility of caring for their aging parents. Three in five caregivers of older adults (ages 50 and older) are women.[91] Although caregiving for parents is commonly divided within a family among sons and daughters, "daughters are more likely to provide basic care and sons are more likely to provide financial assistance," according to a 2011 study by MetLife.[92]

Women Who Are Forced to Work Part Time Earn Less

The flexibility of part-time work can help women balance work and family demands, but that flexibility may come at a cost. The decision to work an alternative or reduced schedule may appear voluntary. However, for many women it is the best option for balancing work with the needs of their family.[93] Roughly two-thirds of part-time workers are women, and women in their prime working years are twice as likely as men to work part time for noneconomic reasons, including child care constraints, family obligations, school enrollment or other reasons.[94]

Part-time workers often face an earnings penalty when compared with their full-time counterparts.[95] Less "face time" can cause employers to view female employees as less committed to their jobs and more likely to take time off to care for family members than their male colleagues. That presumption means that women appear to be less valuable. They receive less pay for work that is substantially similar to men's which in turn contributes to the gender pay gap and the "mommy penalty" phenomenon. Women who work part time are also less likely to qualify for benefits such as paid leave, health insurance and employer-sponsored retirement plans.[96]

Women Tend to Study in Lower-Paying Fields

Over the past several decades, an increasing share of women have earned college and graduate degrees. In the 2012-2013 school year, women earned 57 percent of bachelor's degrees, 60 percent of master's degrees and 51 percent of doctorate degrees.[97] These trends have helped narrow the overall gap between women's and men's earnings.[98]

However, despite the fact that women tend to be better educated than men, women's median earnings are lower at every level of education. In fact, women with bachelor's and professional degrees face *larger* pay gaps than women with less education. For example, while the national gender pay gap is 21 percent, the pay gap for women with a bachelor's degree is 29 percent.[99]

Moreover, women are often out-earned by men who are less educated. For example, a woman with a graduate or professional degree typically earns $5,000 less than the median earnings of a man with only a bachelor's degree.[100]

This discrepancy is partly due to the fact that women are more likely to pursue education in fields that tend to pay substantially less than those chosen by men. Men are more likely to major in fields such as computer science, chemistry, physics or engineering, which frequently lead to higher-paying jobs.[101] Women are more likely to study subjects such as nursing, education and the social sciences, which often lead to lower-paying jobs. For example, women earn more than 60 percent of degrees in nine of the 10 lowest-paying fields of study, but less than 30 percent of degrees in seven of the 10 highest-paying fields (see **Table 2**).

Table 2: College Majors with the Highest and Lowest Earnings					
20 Majors with *Highest* Earnings	**Median Earnings**	**Percent Female**	**20 Majors with *Lowest* Earnings**	**Median Earnings**	**Percent Female**
Petroleum engineering	$136,000	14%	Early childhood education	$39,000	96%
Pharmacy, pharmaceutical sciences & admin.	$113,000	59%	Human services & community organization	$41,000	85%
Metallurgical engineering	$98,000	23%	Studio arts	$42,000	69%
Mining and mineral engineering	$97,000	13%	Social work	$42,000	88%
Chemical engineering	$96,000	32%	Teacher education: multiple levels	$42,000	82%
Electrical engineering	$93,000	12%	Visual & performing arts	$42,000	67%
Aerospace engineering	$90,000	14%	Theology & religious vocations	$43,000	32%
Mechanical engineering	$87,000	12%	Elementary education	$43,000	91%
Computer engineering	$87,000	10%	Drama & theater arts	$45,000	63%
Geological & geophysical engineering	$87,000	40%	Family & consumer sciences	$45,000	90%
Computer science	$83,000	13%	Language & drama education	$45,000	76%
Civil engineering	$83,000	21%	Special needs education	$45,000	90%
Applied mathematics	$83,000	35%	General education	$46,000	83%
Industrial & manufacturing engineering	$81,000	28%	Multi/interdisciplinary studies	$46,000	60%
Physics	$81,000	19%	Art & music education	$46,000	66%
General engineering	$81,000	22%	services	$46,000	95%
Engineering mechanics, physics & science	$81,000	20%	Composition & speech	$47,000	65%
Architectural engineering	$80,000	25%	Social sciences or history teacher education	$47,000	41%
Engineering & industrial management	$78,000	17%	Science & computer teacher education	$48,000	60%
Statistics & decision science	$78,000	44%	Secondary teacher education	$48,000	59%

Source: JEC Democratic staff calculations based on data from the National Center for Education Statistics, 2014 Digest of Education Statistics (women's share of each major is based on degrees conferred during the 2012-13 education year found in Table 318.30); Georgetown University Center on Education and the Workforce (2015), which uses U.S. Census Bureau, American Community Service micro data, 2009 to 2013
Notes: "Median earnings" refers to the median annual wages of college-educated workers ages 25 to 59; earnings in 2013 dollars; majors are matched as closely as possible between earnings data and women's share of degrees

Women continue to be underrepresented in science, technology, engineering and mathematics (STEM), a broad field of study that is typically associated with higher wages. Women today hold less than half (46 percent) of science and engineering degrees, but their representation is growing as more young women pursue education in STEM. Young women (ages 25 to 39 years old), outnumber their male colleagues in science and engineering, 52 percent to 48 percent.[102]

However, even within STEM, women are still more likely to earn degrees in fields that pay less. For example, women earned well over half of bachelor's degrees in biology conferred in the 2012-2013 academic year, a field in which the median salary for bachelor's degree holders is $56,000.[103] On the other hand, women earned less than 20 percent of bachelor's degrees in engineering, a field in which the median salary for bachelor's degree holders is $81,000.[104]

Selecting a major or field of study is largely a personal choice. However, research suggests that even from an early age women are steered into certain fields of study and discouraged from entering others.[105] According to studies, young girls perceive themselves to be worse at math and science than young boys, which makes them less likely to take courses in STEM and pursue education in those higher-paying fields.[106] Additionally, because relatively fewer older women work in higher-paying, male-dominated professions, there are fewer mentors for younger women and girls, decreasing the chance that they will pursue careers in these professions.[107]

Women Often Work in Occupations That Pay Less

Women's median weekly earnings are less than men's in each of the top 20 occupations for female employment. Those occupations employ 19.8 million women and account for more than 42 percent of women's total employment (see **Figure 10**). [108]

Within these 20 occupations, women's earnings range from a high of 99 percent of men's for maids and housekeeping cleaners (men and women earn essentially the same pay) to a low of 67 percent of men's for financial managers (women earn roughly two-thirds of men's pay). Many of the most common occupations for women typically pay salaries below the overall median, and in many cases, below the poverty line for a family of four.[109]

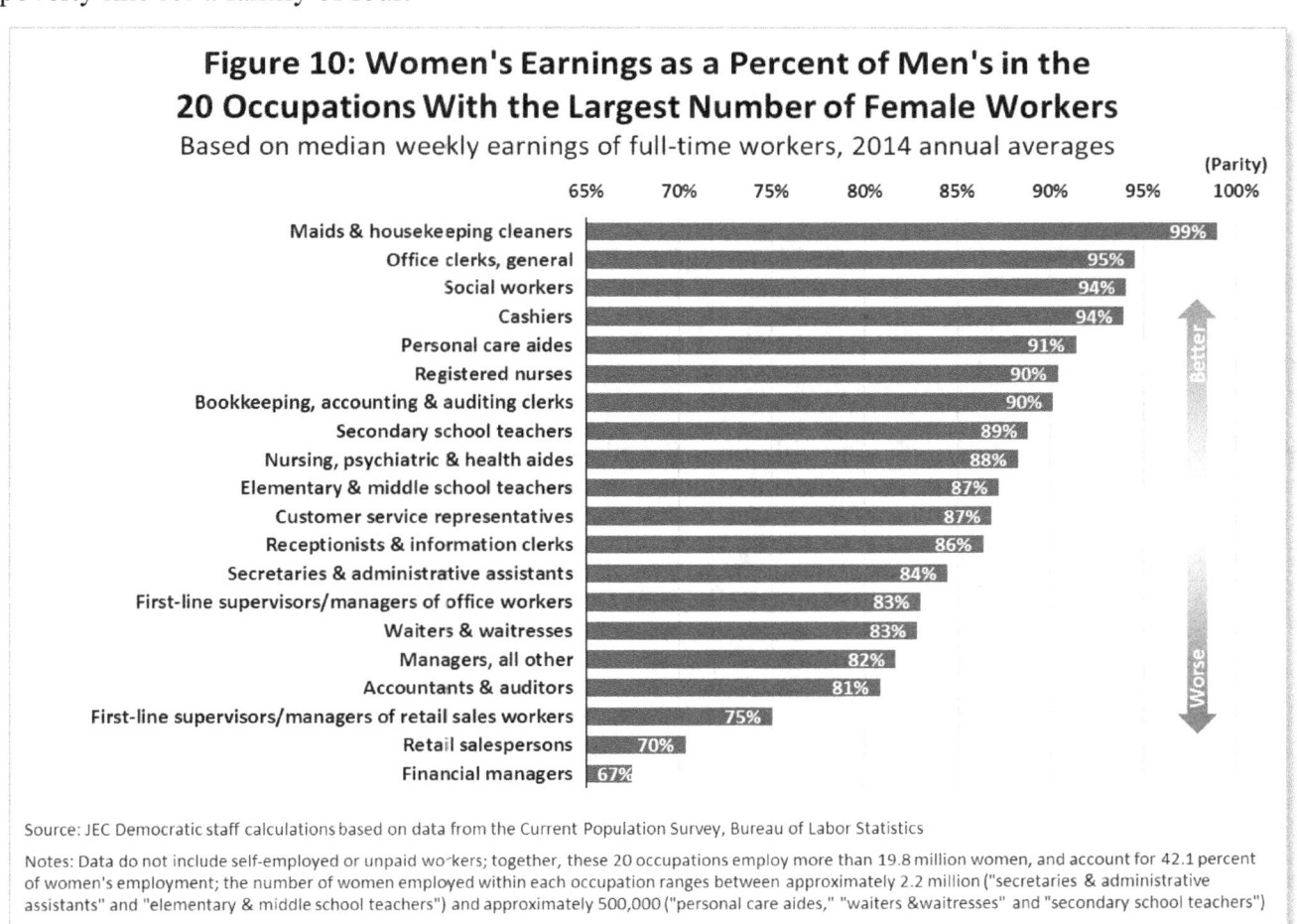

Figure 10: Women's Earnings as a Percent of Men's in the 20 Occupations With the Largest Number of Female Workers

Based on median weekly earnings of full-time workers, 2014 annual averages

Occupation	Percent
Maids & housekeeping cleaners	99%
Office clerks, general	95%
Social workers	94%
Cashiers	94%
Personal care aides	91%
Registered nurses	90%
Bookkeeping, accounting & auditing clerks	90%
Secondary school teachers	89%
Nursing, psychiatric & health aides	88%
Elementary & middle school teachers	87%
Customer service representatives	87%
Receptionists & information clerks	86%
Secretaries & administrative assistants	84%
First-line supervisors/managers of office workers	83%
Waiters & waitresses	83%
Managers, all other	82%
Accountants & auditors	81%
First-line supervisors/managers of retail sales workers	75%
Retail salespersons	70%
Financial managers	67%

Source: JEC Democratic staff calculations based on data from the Current Population Survey, Bureau of Labor Statistics

Notes: Data do not include self-employed or unpaid workers; together, these 20 occupations employ more than 19.8 million women, and account for 42.1 percent of women's employment; the number of women employed within each occupation ranges between approximately 2.2 million ("secretaries & administrative assistants" and "elementary & middle school teachers") and approximately 500,000 ("personal care aides," "waiters &waitresses" and "secondary school teachers")

Women tend to work in professions that overwhelmingly employ females, including nursing, teaching and office and administrative support positions.[110] These professions have traditionally paid lower wages than male-dominated professions.

One factor that contributes to lower wages in female-dominated professions is that many of those professions focus on caregiving, which generally is poorly compensated. "Caring often creates 'outputs' that are not easily captured in market transactions, such as the increases in lifetime capabilities created by excellent kindergarten and preschool teachers," according to economist Nancy Folbre. The added value of such work, "which extends well beyond increases in lifetime earnings to many less tangible benefits," is difficult to quantify. As a result, wages in caregiving professions do not reflect the full value of the work.[111]

The result is that workers—both men and women—in traditionally female occupations face a wage penalty.[112] For example, the median weekly earnings of maids and housekeepers, a category that is 84 percent women, is more than 20 percent lower than the median weekly earnings of janitors and building cleaners, a category that is 76 percent men.[113] According to the Institute for Women's Policy Research, "Male-dominated occupations tend to pay more than female-dominated occupations at similar skill levels, particularly at higher levels of educational attainment."[114]

Of the 116 occupations with enough men and women to make a comparison, women earn as much as or more than men in only two—stock clerks/order fillers and health practitioner support technologists/technicians.[115] A gender wage gap exists within low-paying occupations (for example, cashiers and packagers), as well as within high-paying occupations (such as nurses, accountants and financial managers).[116]

Moreover, women tend to hold larger shares of employment in lower-paying occupations within a particular field—e.g., medicine, law or finance. For example, in the medical field, 90 percent of registered nurses are female, but only 36 percent of physicians and surgeons are female.[117] Similarly, within the field of finance, 90 percent of bookkeepers, accountants and auditing clerks are female, but only about 40 percent of financial analysts and personal financial advisors are female.[118] Within the legal field, where men and women hold roughly equal shares of total employment, women are 87 percent of paralegals and legal assistants, but only 33 percent of lawyers.[119]

Evidence suggests that most women do not choose to work in low-paying jobs in exchange for more flexibility, despite claims by some to the contrary. According to economist Heather Boushey, "…mothers are actually less likely to be employed in jobs that provide greater flexibility. In general, workers who hold higher positions and are privileged in gender (better educated, white, male) have more access to all kinds of workplace flexibility. Women are less likely than men to have access to flexibility, but parents—especially single mothers—are the least likely to have access to workplace flexibility."[120]

In other words, lower-income women who potentially would benefit the most from policies that enhance workplace flexibility are among the least likely to have access to them. Flexible arrangements for low-wage workers are more often in the form of reduced hours (part-time or part-year work) that come with reduced pay. Only 44 percent of low-wage workers (average wage in the bottom 10 percent) have access to paid leave including sick days, family leave and vacation.[121]

Women Are Underrepresented in Leadership

Women hold significantly fewer leadership positions than men, despite being more than half the U.S. population.[122] This is true across both the public and private sectors. Women hold 108 seats in the U.S. Congress—20 seats in the Senate and 88 seats in the House of Representatives (including four nonvoting delegates). Although this is a record number of women serving in the U.S. Congress, it represents only 20 percent of the 539 seats.[123]

Across state governments, women hold just six of the 50 state governorships and only about 25 percent of both statewide elective executive offices (including governor, lieutenant governor and other statewide elected offices) and seats in state legislatures.[124] Only about 18 percent of mayors of cities with more than 30,000 residents are women, and only 17 mayors of the 100 largest cities are women.[125]

Although women make up 48 percent of the private-sector workforce, they comprise only 4 percent of CEOs of S&P 1500 companies, and 16 percent of board members at those companies.[126] That is despite the fact that women's share of board seats has roughly doubled since 1997. According to the Government Accountability Office (GAO), even if the pace at which women join corporate boards more than doubles to match the pace for men, it will be more than 40 years before women and men reach parity.[127]

Women tend to hold more board seats at large companies than at small and medium-sized companies. In fact, one in three small-sized companies, and roughly one in six medium-sized companies have no female representation on their corporate board.[128]

Multiple factors likely play a role in the lack of gender diversity on corporate boards.[129] Boards may not prioritize diversity when filling corporate board seats, or there may be an unconscious bias against women in order to maintain a "level of comfort in the boardroom," according to interviews conducted by GAO of stakeholders including CEOs, board directors and investors. Among small and medium S&P 1500 companies, the median number of female board members is one. Among large companies, the median number is two.[130]

Other factors that hinder increasing women's representation in corporate leadership include a lower percentage of women in the traditional pathway for leadership positions, and the fact that there is generally low turnover among board members.[131]

Increasing women's representation in corporate leadership may boost companies' bottom lines. Multiple studies have suggested that gender diversity in corporate leadership is linked to improved financial performance.[132] Moreover, diverse boards often better reflect the composition of a given company's pool of employees, as well as its customer base. Increasing diversity on corporate boards also can lead to better decision-making by allowing members to consider a greater range of perspectives.[133]

Evidence Suggests That Some Women Still Do Not Receive "Equal Pay for Equal Work"

In many professions, women continue to be paid less for doing work that is substantially the same as work done by men. For example, among nurses, women make 90 percent of what men typically make; among lawyers, women make 83 percent of what men make; and among financial managers women make roughly 67 percent of what men make.[134] This suggests that there may still be gender-based discrimination in the workplace.

After taking into account differences in observable factors such as education, field of study, occupation and experience, multiple studies have estimated that there is an unaccounted for gap between women's and men's average earnings of 5 to 9 percent.[135] In other words, as much as 40 percent of the overall gender pay gap cannot be explained by factors that would affect earnings and may be due to discrimination.

A 2011 study by the American Association of University Women found that one year after graduating from similar universities, with the same major, and working the same number of hours, female employees earned 7 percent less than male employees.[136] That unexplained difference grew in subsequent years, reaching 12 percent a decade after graduation.[137]

Similarly, a recent study by Francine D. Blau and Lawrence M. Kahn estimated that about 40 percent of the difference in earnings between full-time working men and women—or roughly 8 cents on the dollar—was unexplained by measurable gender differences in education, experience, region, race, union status, industry and occupation.[138] Another study, which used slightly different data on earnings, found an unexplained shortfall in women's earnings of approximately 5 to 7 cents for each dollar earned by a man.[139]

INTERNATIONAL COMPARISONS

The United States now ranks 28th on the World Economic Forum's (WEF) Global Gender Gap Index, not only behind many developed countries, but also behind developing countries such as Rwanda, Nicaragua and Namibia. This ranking is down eight spots from a year earlier. The rankings are based on four fundamental categories compiled by the WEF that measure each country's performance relating to various aspects of women's well-being and opportunity, including economic participation, education, health and political empowerment. Much of the drop in the U.S. ranking was due to a decline in the political empowerment score, but the United States also lost its spot as one of the top five countries for economic participation and opportunity, "with slightly less wage equality for similar work."[140]

The United States not only lags behind many other advanced countries with respect to reducing gender wage inequality, it also lags behind other countries in adopting family-friendly policies that could help address some of the factors that influence the pay gap. These policies, including paid family leave, universal child care, workplace flexibility and retirement benefits for unpaid caregivers, make it easier for both women and men to balance the often-competing demands of work and family.

The Gender Pay Gap Is Larger in the United States Than in Many Other Developed Countries

Comparing gender pay inequality across countries is difficult due to significant differences in employment patterns and the lack of publicly available data on wage disparities in some countries. This leaves some question about where the United States ranks in the world with respect to gender pay equity, but by and large, the consensus is that it fairs poorly.

Several studies have concluded that the gender pay gap in the United States is larger than in many other advanced countries.[141] For example, the United States ranks 23rd among OECD countries when comparing women's median wages for full-time work to men's. In other words, the gap between women's and men's wages in the United States is greater than it is in 22 of 34 developed countries in the OECD (see **Figure 11**).

The good news is that the factors that account for a significant portion of the gender pay gap in the United States are known and could be addressed. As discussed earlier, these include differences in fields of study, occupations and experience. Implementing policies targeted to narrowing those differences could significantly shrink the gender pay gap. That includes embracing solutions to minimize subtle forms of gender discrimination such as occupational segregation, and maximizing the economic potential of U.S. women through policies such as paid family leave and affordable child care.

Figure 11: Gender Wage Gap in Selected Countries

Source: Organisation for Economic Co-operation and Development, Gender Wage Gap 2014

Notes: Data for each country are for the most recent year available; OECD defines the gender wage gap as unadjusted and as the difference between male and female median wages divided by male median wages; data are for full-time employees

The United States Is the Only Advanced Country That Does Not Guarantee Paid Maternity Leave

The United States is one of a small number of countries and the only advanced nation that does not guarantee paid maternity leave for working mothers.[142] In every other advanced country, new mothers are entitled to a period of paid leave, although the duration of leave and the portion of leave that is paid vary considerably across countries. According to the International Labour Organization, 53 percent of all countries provide at least 14 weeks of maternity leave.[143] Paid paternity leave is less common. Sweden has an exceptionally generous parental leave policy for mothers and fathers, providing 480 days of paid parental leave, with 60 of those days reserved for the father.[144]

Given the wide variation in leave policies across countries, the optimal duration of paid parental leave is unclear. It is certainly longer than the zero weeks currently guaranteed in the United States. However, according to an OECD analysis, in some countries with extremely long durations of paid parental leave, such as Austria and Finland, women face larger gender pay gaps.[145] This is due to the fact that women who take the full maternity leave benefit available to them may be out of the workforce for an extended period of time, and those long breaks in work are linked to lower earnings.[146]

Increasing the availability and use of paid parental leave for fathers in the United States, as other countries have done, also would help combat long-standing gender stereotypes with respect to unpaid work and caregiving. In countries including Sweden, France, Belgium, Denmark and Finland, a portion of parental leave is reserved for fathers.[147]

Family-friendly workplace policies that apply only to women such as paid maternity leave may unintentionally reinforce the stereotype that women should be their family's primary caregiver. Women in general devote more time to unpaid work, including child care, and such policies can make it more likely that women leave the labor force for long periods of time, which can in turn perpetuate pay disparities.[148]

Breaking those stereotypes could shrink the gender pay gap two ways: first, by lessening the stigma some men feel for taking leave, and second, by making it less likely that employers undervalue women as a result of their caregiving responsibilities. In addition, parents would more equally share in the unpaid work of childrearing. A 2007 study of U.S. working fathers found that those who stayed home for at least two weeks following the arrival of a child were significantly more likely to share in child care responsibilities nine months later.[149]

Several U.S. companies have taken steps to increase the likelihood that fathers take paid leave following the arrival of a child. Facebook and Etsy have recently updated their parental leave policies to provide equal benefits to all new parents, regardless of gender. Other companies have expanded their parental leave policies to include paid leave explicitly for fathers or secondary caregivers.

The United States Is One of Only a Few Countries Without A Paid Sick Leave Policy

Workers in most countries, including those in low-income countries such as Afghanistan, Ethiopia and Haiti, are entitled to paid leave when they are sick.[150] However, the United States does not have a nationwide paid sick leave policy. Five states—Connecticut, Massachusetts, Oregon, California and Vermont—and the District of Columbia have already enacted paid sick leave laws.[151] An additional 22 cities and one county have also passed paid sick leave legislation.[152] The experiences in these states and cities have shown that providing workers with paid sick leave does not hurt businesses' bottom lines. In fact, it can have positive effects on worker productivity and boost employee morale.[153]

Despite this progress, roughly 35 percent of U.S. workers do not have access to paid sick leave.[154] Access is higher among workers in high-wage and full-time jobs. Part-time and low-wage workers— who are often female—are less likely to have access to paid sick leave. Roughly 80 percent of the lowest-wage workers do not have access to paid sick leave. By comparison, only one in 10 of the highest-wage workers lack access to paid sick leave.[155] Nearly three-quarters of part-time workers do not have paid sick leave.[156]

The United States Has the Third Highest Out-of-Pocket Child Care Costs in the OECD

Parents in the United States pay very high costs for reliable child care. In 33 states and the District of Columbia, the annual cost of child care for an infant exceeds the cost of a year of in-state tuition at a four-year public university.[157] For many families, the high cost of child care pushes mothers out of the labor force until their children are old enough to attend public pre-K or kindergarten. Those years out of the workforce have long-term effects on mothers' career earnings and retirement security.

According to the OECD, the United States ranks near the bottom for public spending on child care and pre-primary education as a share of the economy. At just 0.4 percent of gross domestic product, U.S. expenditures were about half the OECD average.[158] The lack of public spending leaves American families with high out-of-pocket costs. By one measure, the United States has the third highest out-of-pocket costs for child care among OECD countries.[159]

Many countries, and European nations in particular, have adopted policies to improve child care access and affordability. For example, in France several policies are aimed at ensuring that families have access to affordable and reliable child care, including affordable municipal day care, tax breaks for hiring in-home child care workers and free universal preschool beginning at 3 years of age.[160] In the United Kingdom, working parents of 3- and 4-year-olds receive 30 hours of free child care per week, and the most disadvantaged families of 2-year-olds receive child care at no cost.[161]

Many High-Income Countries Have Laws to Encourage Workplace Flexibility

Many countries have flexible workplace statutes that help employees achieve work-life balance by requiring or encouraging employers to allow alternative work arrangements, such as scheduling changes due to child care responsibilities. A comparison among the United States and other high-income countries published by the Institute for Women's Policy Research in 2008 showed that around that time, nearly all of the 20 other countries studied had flexible workplace policies to accommodate child care needs and about one-third had policies to accommodate care for a sick or elderly adult.[162]

Research by economist Claudia Goldin suggests that increasing "temporal flexibility" so that jobs are structured to give workers more autonomy over their schedules, and so workers can more easily substitute for each other, could reduce the gender pay gap. However, in many professions, including in high-paying fields such as the corporate, financial and legal fields, "a flexible schedule comes at a high price," according to Goldin, because workers in these fields often get a disproportionately large increase in their pay for working additional hours.[163] While some fields have worked toward reducing the cost of workplace flexibility to employees (pharmacy and retail sales, for example), workers in many professions continue to face large penalties when they elect to work non-standard schedules.[164]

Many European Countries Place a Value on Caregiving

Time spent out of the workforce to care for children and other family members significantly impacts women's earnings and retirement security. Some countries have found ways to value the time parents spend caring for their families and recognize the role parents play in developing human capital and shaping the future workforce.[165] For example, they give credit to women (or men) for time spent out of the workforce to care for children or other relatives. These types of programs exist in many European countries including France, Germany, Sweden, Norway, Switzerland, Luxembourg, Austria and Finland.[166] Adopting similar policies to value the time individuals spend on unpaid caregiving in the United States could help reduced the costs of caregiving to women, particularly in retirement.[167]

Many Countries Require Pay Transparency to Address Their Gender Pay Gaps

The vast majority of OECD countries, including the United States, have legislated the principle of "equal pay for equal work" into law. Many have also adopted laws that guarantee equal pay for "work of equal value requiring similar qualifications." In addition, protecting the right of workers to share salary information with coworkers is essential for ensuring that men and women receive fair pay.

Disclosing overall statistics on pay can be a useful tool for uncovering broader underlying inequities in compensation practices. Several countries have enacted laws requiring private companies to periodically disclose their gender pay gaps. For example, every two years, companies in Belgium with 50 or more employees must report differences in pay between men and women in their annual audit.[168] Similar laws are already in place in Sweden and Austria, and an equal pay reporting requirement for companies with at least 250 employees is being considered in the United Kingdom.[169]

The U.S. federal government is also taking steps to bolster available data on workers' pay to help identify and address pay discrimination. Subject to final approval, the U.S. Equal Employment Opportunity Commission (EEOC) will begin collecting additional data on pay ranges and hours worked from private-sector employers with more than 100 employees beginning in 2017 to assess pay disparities across industries and occupations by sex, race and ethnicity.[170]

THE STATUS OF "EQUAL PAY FOR EQUAL WORK"

Congress Passed the Lilly Ledbetter Fair Pay Act to Help Ensure "Equal Pay for Equal Work"

Congress took steps to strengthen protections against pay discrimination by passing the **Lilly Ledbetter Fair Pay Act** in 2009. It was the first piece of legislation President Obama signed into law, and it addressed a major shortcoming of existing equal pay laws—the fact that many victims are not aware of pay discrimination until it is too late to take action.

The law is named for Lilly Ledbetter, a nearly 20-year employee of Goodyear Tire and Rubber. Late in her career, Ledbetter discovered that she had been paid significantly less than her male counterparts—more than $200,000 in salary over the course of her career, and more in Social Security and pension benefits. Upon retirement, she sued her employer for gender discrimination and her case ultimately reached the Supreme Court. In a 5-4 decision, the Supreme Court ruled that employers could not be sued for an unlawful practice more than 180 days after the initial alleged discrimination had occurred.

However, as is often the case with pay discrimination, Ledbetter did not learn she was being discriminated against until long after the 180-day period had expired.

The Lilly Ledbetter Act addressed this by revising the Civil Rights Act so that the 180-day statute of limitations for filing a pay discrimination lawsuit resets with each new paycheck. According to the Equal Employment Opportunity Commission, gender-based wage discrimination charges and Equal Pay Act charge filings both increased following enactment of the law.[171]

Passing the Paycheck Fairness Act Would Further Strengthen Pay Equity Laws

The **Paycheck Fairness Act** would address several significant holes in the Equal Pay Act of 1963 that enable discriminatory pay practices to continue. If enacted, the bill would make several changes that would further strengthen pay equity laws.[172] The Paycheck Fairness Act would require that wage comparisons be made across multiple establishments within the same county or political jurisdiction under the same employer. Currently, employers are only required to compare wages of men and women doing the same job at the same establishment. This means a woman can be paid less than a man who is doing the same job, but "across town."

The bill also would prohibit employers from defending unequal pay for "equal work" for reasons that are not directly related to job content and performance. Some employers have successfully defended paying a woman less than a man for doing the same job on the basis of an individual's prior pay history or stronger negotiation for higher pay. Moreover, employers would be prohibited from punishing workers for sharing pay information with colleagues. Increasing pay transparency would help all employees access the information they need to ensure they are being paid fairly. And it is essential for women to be able to fight against discriminatory pay practices. Without it, uncovering and proving pay discrimination can be challenging, time-consuming and costly. Yet, over 60 percent of private-sector workers report that they have been discouraged or prohibited from discussing information on pay.[173]

The Paycheck Fairness Act would require the Equal Employment Opportunity Commission to collect data on employer compensation across race, sex and national origin, and enhance the EEOC's ability to enforce anti-discrimination laws. Remedy provisions in the Equal Pay Act would be strengthened to include compensatory and punitive damages. The more stringent penalties would encourage employers to self-audit and more quickly correct any discriminatory pay practices as they are uncovered.

The ERA Would Put the Full Weight of the Constitution Behind Anti-Discrimination Laws

Many countries guarantee women have equal rights in their constitutions or other governing documents, including developed countries such as Canada, Japan, and Germany, as well as developing countries such as Afghanistan, Cambodia and Haiti.[174] There may be flaws in how such rights are protected and enforced within a country, but nevertheless, equality is on the books. The U.S. Constitution does not explicitly guarantee that the rights it protects are held equally by all citizens, regardless of sex.[175]

The **Equal Rights Amendment** (ERA), which was first introduced in Congress nearly 93 years ago, would amend the Constitution to ensure that women and men have constitutionally guaranteed equal rights.[176] It would put the full weight of the U.S. Constitution behind existing laws that protect women from discrimination based on sex, including the Equal Pay Act and the Civil Rights Act. Ratifying the ERA would also affirm the United States' position as a leader on women's equality. In 1972, the last time Congress passed and sent the ERA to the states for ratification, 35 states eventually approved the measure—three states short of the 38 needed to amend the Constitution.[177]

Many states have already gone beyond the current federal anti-discrimination laws to advance and protect women's rights by providing either inclusive or partial guarantees of equal rights on the basis of sex in their constitutions.[178]

However, until the ERA is ratified, the progress toward women's equality can be undone. Federal anti-discrimination laws, including the Equal Pay Act and Civil Rights Act, may be amended or repealed. Moreover, future administrations could choose not to enforce them.[179]

CONCLUSION

The Equal Pay Act of 1963 was a monumental step for addressing gender-based discrimination in the workplace by mandating equal pay for equal work. But gender discrimination in the workplace still exists, in both explicit and subtle forms. Despite progress on narrowing the gender pay gap since the 1960s, women still earn less than $4 for every $5 earned by men.

Since Congress passed the Equal Pay Act, there has been a dramatic shift in women's roles in the labor force and as their family's breadwinner. Yet workplace policies have not kept pace, and many women are forced to sacrifice their career to care for their family. This reality depresses women's earnings, contributing to gender pay inequality and pushing some women into poverty.

Unless something changes, the gender pay gap will not be closed for at least 43 years. Women and their families cannot afford to wait that long. Strengthening anti-discrimination laws and modernizing outdated workplace policies to reflect 21st century realities would help women to reach their full economic potential and could significantly shrink the gender pay gap. This would have enormous benefits for women, their families and the economy.

APPENDICES

Methodology: Why Some Sources Quote Different Figures for the Gender Pay Gap

The U.S. government has produced data on men's and women's earnings for over 50 years.[180] Those data are frequently used by economists to compare the median earnings of men and women—the value at the middle of the distribution of men's earnings with the value at the middle of the distribution of women's earnings. This provides an estimate of the size of the gender pay gap. Comparisons can be made between men and women overall, by race or by age, and within specific fields or occupations.

The most frequently cited estimate of the gender pay gap is calculated using annual earnings for individuals who work full time, year-round.[181] This methodology, which gives a *female-to-male earnings ratio* of 78.6 percent and a *gender pay gap* of 21.4 percent, is useful because it excludes the earnings of part-time workers, and includes other forms of pay such as tips, commissions and bonuses. Consistent data are available as far back as 1960, before the passage of the Equal Pay Act, making it possible to track changes in the pay gap over a long period of time.[182]

Other measures of earnings, which did not exist before the 1970s, yield somewhat different results. Comparing median *weekly* earnings, which includes individuals who work full time, finds a female-to-male earnings ratio of 82.5 percent, or a pay gap of 17.5 percent.[183] Comparing *hourly* earnings shows an earnings ratio of 84.6 percent and a pay gap of 15.4 percent.[184] This measure includes individuals who are paid on an hourly basis but may not work full time or year-round. As a result, calculating the pay gap on the basis of hourly earnings captures the many women who work part time or part year. However, this ignores the reality that many women work part time or part year while they are caring for children or other relatives even though they would prefer full-time work.

There is general agreement that no single measure of earnings captures the full range of factors that contribute to the gender pay gap. Regardless, these measures all show that women typically earn less than men.[185]

Table: State-Level Earnings and Pay Gap (2014)

Appendix Table: Gender Earnings Ratio by State (114th Congress)				
	Women's Median Earnings	Men's Median Earnings	Gender Earnings Ratio	Gender Pay Gap
Alabama	$32,100	$44,200	72.6%	27.4%
Alaska	$46,300	$57,300	80.8%	19.2%
Arizona	$36,900	$43,900	84.1%	15.9%
Arkansas	$31,200	$39,900	78.2%	21.8%
California	$42,500	$50,500	84.2%	15.8%
Colorado	$41,700	$50,900	81.9%	18.1%
Connecticut	$50,700	$61,400	82.6%	17.4%
Delaware	$41,300	$51,000	81.0%	19.0%
District of Columbia	$61,700	$68,900	89.6%	10.4%
Florida	$34,800	$41,000	84.9%	15.1%
Georgia	$36,500	$44,600	81.8%	18.2%
Hawaii	$40,200	$46,800	85.9%	14.1%
Idaho	$31,000	$42,600	72.8%	27.2%
Illinois	$40,900	$51,700	79.1%	20.9%
Indiana	$34,800	$46,300	75.2%	24.8%
Iowa	$36,500	$47,200	77.3%	22.7%
Kansas	$36,200	$47,000	77.0%	23.0%
Kentucky	$33,700	$42,200	79.9%	20.1%
Louisiana	$31,600	$48,400	65.3%	34.7%
Maine	$36,100	$45,800	78.8%	21.2%
Maryland	$50,500	$59,100	85.4%	14.6%
Massachusetts	$50,500	$61,600	82.0%	18.0%
Michigan	$37,400	$50,200	74.5%	25.5%
Minnesota	$42,100	$51,600	81.6%	18.4%
Mississippi	$31,500	$40,900	77.0%	23.0%
Missouri	$35,300	$45,600	77.4%	22.6%
Montana	$31,700	$42,700	74.2%	25.8%
Nebraska	$35,100	$44,500	78.9%	21.1%
Nevada	$36,000	$42,300	85.1%	14.9%
New Hampshire	$42,100	$55,600	75.7%	24.3%
New Jersey	$48,900	$60,900	80.3%	19.7%
New Mexico	$32,500	$41,600	78.1%	21.9%
New York	$44,800	$51,600	86.8%	13.2%
North Carolina	$35,500	$41,900	84.7%	15.3%
North Dakota	$36,100	$50,600	71.3%	28.7%
Ohio	$37,100	$47,700	77.8%	22.2%
Oklahoma	$32,200	$43,800	73.5%	26.5%
Oregon	$38,800	$47,200	82.2%	17.8%
Pennsylvania	$39,900	$50,400	79.2%	20.8%
Puerto Rico	$22,900	$21,900	104.6%	-4.6%
Rhode Island	$41,500	$50,800	81.7%	18.3%
South Carolina	$33,700	$42,000	80.2%	19.8%
South Dakota	$32,000	$42,000	76.2%	23.8%
Tennessee	$34,000	$41,700	81.5%	18.5%
Texas	$36,400	$46,200	78.8%	21.2%
Utah	$34,400	$50,900	67.6%	32.4%
Vermont	$39,300	$46,900	83.8%	16.2%
Virginia	$42,400	$52,900	80.2%	19.8%
Washington	$41,900	$54,400	77.0%	23.0%
West Virginia	$31,700	$45,300	70.0%	30.0%
Wisconsin	$37,500	$47,500	78.9%	21.1%
Wyoming	$35,700	$51,900	68.8%	31.2%

Source: JEC Democratic staff calculations based on data from the U.S. Census Bureau, 2014 American Community Survey (1-year estimates) using American FactFinder

Notes: Data are based on median annual earnings of those who have worked full time, year-round in the past 12 months; earnings data are in 2014 inflation-adjusted dollars, rounded to nearest hundred dollars; population 16 years and over with earnings

Map: Gender Earnings Ratio by Congressional District (114th Congress)

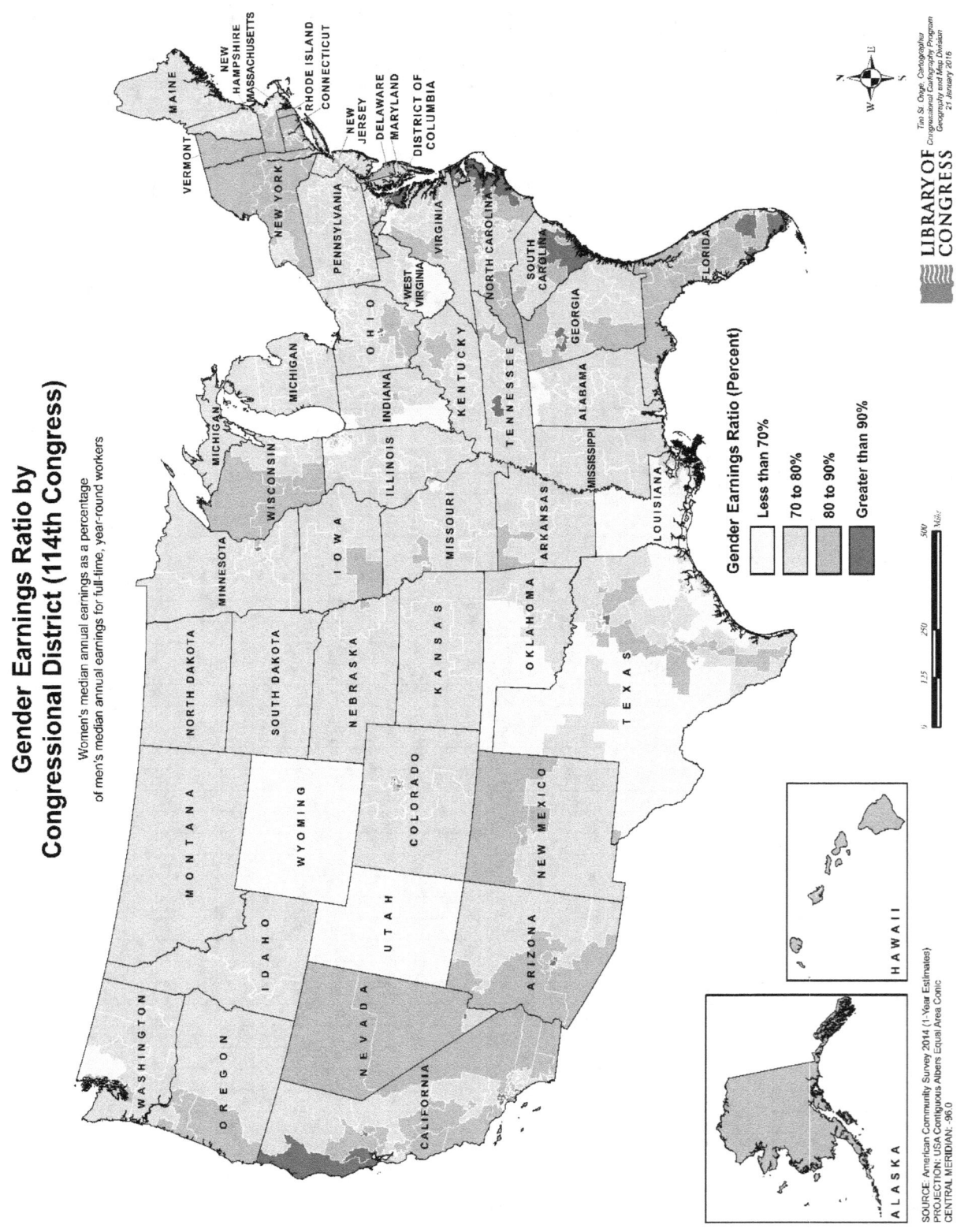

Gender Earnings Ratio by Congressional District (114th Congress)

Women's median annual earnings as a percentage of men's median annual earnings for full-time, year-round workers

Gender Earnings Ratio (Percent)

Less than 70%
70 to 80%
80 to 90%
Greater than 90%

Tin Si Onge, Cartographer
Congressional Cartography Program
Geography and Map Division
21 January 2016

LIBRARY OF CONGRESS

SOURCE: American Community Survey 2014 (1-Year Estimates)
PROJECTION: USA Contiguous Albers Equal Area Conic
CENTRAL MERIDIAN: -96.0

Table: Gender Pay Gap by Congressional District (114th Congress)

Appendix Table: Gender Pay Gap by Congressional District (114th Congress)

Congressional District	Women's Median Earnings	Men's Median Earnings	Gender Earnings Ratio	Gender Pay Gap
Alabama				
Congressional District 1	$32,400	$45,500	71.3%	28.7%
Congressional District 2	$31,200	$41,700	74.7%	25.3%
Congressional District 3	$31,400	$41,700	75.3%	24.7%
Congressional District 4	$30,000	$40,500	74.1%	25.9%
Congressional District 5	$35,100	$50,100	70.0%	30.0%
Congressional District 6	$38,500	$52,300	73.6%	26.4%
Congressional District 7	$27,500	$36,400	75.5%	24.5%
Alaska				
Congressional District (at Large)	$46,300	$57,300	80.8%	19.2%
Arizona				
Congressional District 1	$35,500	$45,100	78.7%	21.3%
Congressional District 2	$35,100	$44,400	79.1%	20.9%
Congressional District 3	$31,300	$36,300	86.4%	13.6%
Congressional District 4	$33,000	$40,400	81.7%	18.3%
Congressional District 5	$42,300	$56,400	75.0%	25.0%
Congressional District 6	$44,800	$55,300	80.9%	19.1%
Congressional District 7	$31,000	$31,200	99.5%	0.5%
Congressional District 8	$41,000	$50,900	80.5%	19.5%
Congressional District 9	$38,200	$42,200	90.5%	9.5%
Arkansas				
Congressional District 1	$29,700	$37,400	79.5%	20.5%
Congressional District 2	$32,900	$41,800	78.8%	21.2%
Congressional District 3	$35,100	$39,700	88.5%	11.5%
Congressional District 4	$27,200	$38,200	71.1%	28.9%
California				
Congressional District 1	$36,300	$48,400	75.0%	25.0%
Congressional District 2	$50,600	$54,900	92.2%	7.8%
Congressional District 3	$42,200	$50,200	84.0%	16.0%
Congressional District 4	$50,300	$65,600	76.7%	23.3%
Congressional District 5	$47,400	$52,200	90.9%	9.1%
Congressional District 6	$41,500	$43,700	95.0%	5.0%
Congressional District 7	$49,100	$57,100	86.0%	14.0%
Congressional District 8	$37,000	$42,900	86.2%	13.8%
Congressional District 9	$41,600	$50,400	82.7%	17.3%
Congressional District 10	$37,800	$48,100	78.5%	21.5%
Congressional District 11	$52,500	$62,300	84.2%	15.8%
Congressional District 12	$64,300	$76,300	84.2%	15.8%
Congressional District 13	$50,500	$57,100	88.5%	11.5%
Congressional District 14	$54,900	$62,000	88.7%	11.3%
Congressional District 15	$55,200	$70,600	78.1%	21.9%

Appendix Table: Gender Pay Gap by Congressional District (114th Congress)

Congressional District	Women's Median Earnings	Men's Median Earnings	Gender Earnings Ratio	Gender Pay Gap
California (continued)				
Congressional District 16	$30,800	$35,000	87.8%	12.2%
Congressional District 17	$60,000	$91,200	65.8%	34.2%
Congressional District 18	$71,100	$100,300	70.9%	29.1%
Congressional District 19	$47,600	$55,800	85.3%	14.7%
Congressional District 20	$39,200	$45,600	86.1%	13.9%
Congressional District 21	$26,500	$31,300	84.8%	15.2%
Congressional District 22	$37,200	$44,200	84.2%	15.8%
Congressional District 23	$41,000	$52,700	77.9%	22.1%
Congressional District 24	$40,500	$50,500	80.3%	19.7%
Congressional District 25	$45,500	$59,600	76.4%	23.6%
Congressional District 26	$41,800	$52,200	80.1%	19.9%
Congressional District 27	$45,600	$51,100	89.2%	10.8%
Congressional District 28	$46,900	$50,900	92.0%	8.0%
Congressional District 29	$31,400	$33,700	93.0%	7.0%
Congressional District 30	$51,100	$52,400	97.4%	2.6%
Congressional District 31	$40,500	$46,200	87.7%	12.3%
Congressional District 32	$33,700	$40,400	83.4%	16.6%
Congressional District 33	$68,500	$100,100	68.4%	31.6%
Congressional District 34	$27,300	$26,400	103.4%	-3.4%
Congressional District 35	$33,900	$38,400	88.2%	11.8%
Congressional District 36	$32,500	$38,600	84.1%	15.9%
Congressional District 37	$42,200	$42,000	100.5%	-0.5%
Congressional District 38	$37,100	$43,600	85.1%	14.9%
Congressional District 39	$48,200	$55,500	87.0%	13.0%
Congressional District 40	$25,300	$27,100	93.4%	6.6%
Congressional District 41	$32,200	$41,100	78.3%	21.7%
Congressional District 42	$42,100	$58,900	71.4%	28.6%
Congressional District 43	$38,500	$38,300	100.5%	-0.5%
Congressional District 44	$29,200	$32,200	90.7%	9.3%
Congressional District 45	$55,400	$76,400	72.6%	27.4%
Congressional District 46	$31,200	$32,100	97.2%	2.8%
Congressional District 47	$42,600	$49,400	86.2%	13.8%
Congressional District 48	$52,200	$65,100	80.1%	19.9%
Congressional District 49	$44,800	$56,000	79.9%	20.1%
Congressional District 50	$43,900	$50,200	87.3%	12.7%
Congressional District 51	$29,900	$35,700	83.9%	16.1%
Congressional District 52	$57,300	$70,200	81.5%	18.5%
Congressional District 53	$45,900	$51,800	88.5%	11.5%
Colorado				
Congressional District 1	$45,800	$47,200	97.1%	2.9%

Appendix Table: Gender Pay Gap by Congressional District (114th Congress)

Congressional District	Women's Median Earnings	Men's Median Earnings	Gender Earnings Ratio	Gender Pay Gap
Colorado (continued)				
Congressional District 2	$45,300	$56,700	79.9%	20.1%
Congressional District 3	$35,100	$47,000	74.7%	25.3%
Congressional District 4	$41,700	$52,200	79.9%	20.1%
Congressional District 5	$38,700	$49,400	78.3%	21.7%
Congressional District 6	$45,900	$55,300	83.0%	17.0%
Congressional District 7	$41,300	$47,300	87.3%	12.7%
Connecticut				
Congressional District 1	$49,900	$61,700	80.8%	19.2%
Congressional District 2	$50,000	$57,000	87.8%	12.2%
Congressional District 3	$50,100	$60,000	83.4%	16.6%
Congressional District 4	$60,200	$75,200	80.0%	20.0%
Congressional District 5	$50,000	$60,100	83.2%	16.8%
Delaware				
Congressional District (at Large)	$41,300	$51,000	81.0%	19.0%
District of Columbia				
Delegate	$61,700	$68,900	89.5%	10.5%
Florida				
Congressional District 1	$32,000	$42,200	75.8%	24.2%
Congressional District 2	$34,100	$40,400	84.4%	15.6%
Congressional District 3	$35,800	$42,100	84.9%	15.1%
Congressional District 4	$37,700	$46,700	80.8%	19.2%
Congressional District 5	$27,700	$32,200	86.1%	13.9%
Congressional District 6	$36,700	$41,400	88.5%	11.5%
Congressional District 7	$36,500	$43,500	83.9%	16.1%
Congressional District 8	$35,700	$45,600	78.2%	21.8%
Congressional District 9	$31,300	$35,600	87.9%	12.1%
Congressional District 10	$37,600	$44,100	85.1%	14.9%
Congressional District 11	$31,300	$37,800	82.9%	17.1%
Congressional District 12	$39,700	$51,100	77.8%	22.2%
Congressional District 13	$36,600	$41,100	89.0%	11.0%
Congressional District 14	$35,300	$40,200	87.9%	12.1%
Congressional District 15	$35,700	$42,800	83.3%	16.7%
Congressional District 16	$35,500	$41,800	85.0%	15.0%
Congressional District 17	$31,400	$37,500	83.9%	16.1%
Congressional District 18	$36,900	$44,600	82.6%	17.4%
Congressional District 19	$36,600	$40,200	91.2%	8.8%
Congressional District 20	$30,400	$31,800	95.6%	4.4%
Congressional District 21	$40,100	$47,600	84.2%	15.8%
Congressional District 22	$41,400	$46,100	89.9%	10.1%
Congressional District 23	$38,000	$50,500	75.4%	24.6%

Appendix Table: Gender Pay Gap by Congressional District (114th Congress)

Congressional District	Women's Median Earnings	Men's Median Earnings	Gender Earnings Ratio	Gender Pay Gap
Florida (continued)				
Congressional District 24	$30,300	$32,800	92.5%	7.5%
Congressional District 25	$32,000	$36,600	87.5%	12.5%
Congressional District 26	$34,000	$36,400	93.3%	6.7%
Congressional District 27	$30,900	$35,000	88.3%	11.7%
Georgia				
Congressional District 1	$32,600	$41,900	77.7%	22.3%
Congressional District 2	$30,300	$36,900	82.2%	17.8%
Congressional District 3	$35,800	$46,900	76.3%	23.7%
Congressional District 4	$36,800	$40,700	90.5%	9.5%
Congressional District 5	$41,900	$50,000	83.8%	16.2%
Congressional District 6	$50,900	$70,200	72.6%	27.4%
Congressional District 7	$40,300	$50,400	79.9%	20.1%
Congressional District 8	$30,800	$40,700	75.6%	24.4%
Congressional District 9	$31,900	$36,900	86.5%	13.5%
Congressional District 10	$34,100	$44,300	77.0%	23.0%
Congressional District 11	$41,800	$56,300	74.2%	25.8%
Congressional District 12	$30,800	$39,700	77.5%	22.5%
Congressional District 13	$39,200	$41,600	94.1%	5.9%
Congressional District 14	$32,200	$37,800	85.2%	14.8%
Hawaii				
Congressional District 1	$41,000	$50,300	81.6%	18.4%
Congressional District 2	$38,400	$43,600	88.0%	12.0%
Idaho				
Congressional District 1	$31,100	$43,600	71.2%	28.8%
Congressional District 2	$30,900	$42,000	73.7%	26.3%
Illinois				
Congressional District 1	$41,100	$50,900	80.8%	19.2%
Congressional District 2	$38,200	$48,100	79.5%	20.5%
Congressional District 3	$40,700	$51,100	79.7%	20.3%
Congressional District 4	$31,500	$32,000	98.4%	1.6%
Congressional District 5	$51,100	$61,600	83.0%	17.0%
Congressional District 6	$50,900	$71,400	71.3%	28.7%
Congressional District 7	$47,400	$58,600	80.8%	19.2%
Congressional District 8	$41,000	$50,100	81.9%	18.1%
Congressional District 9	$51,500	$56,800	90.6%	9.4%
Congressional District 10	$45,300	$59,100	76.6%	23.4%
Congressional District 11	$41,800	$54,300	76.9%	23.1%
Congressional District 12	$35,900	$46,700	76.9%	23.1%
Congressional District 13	$36,100	$48,000	75.3%	24.7%
Congressional District 14	$46,800	$67,700	69.2%	30.8%

Appendix Table: Gender Pay Gap by Congressional District (114th Congress)

Congressional District	Women's Median Earnings	Men's Median Earnings	Gender Earnings Ratio	Gender Pay Gap
Illinois (continued)				
Congressional District 15	$32,100	$44,700	71.8%	28.2%
Congressional District 16	$36,300	$51,600	70.3%	29.7%
Congressional District 17	$31,900	$44,200	72.1%	27.9%
Congressional District 18	$38,100	$51,900	73.4%	26.6%
Indiana				
Congressional District 1	$35,900	$52,400	68.4%	31.6%
Congressional District 2	$31,300	$42,100	74.4%	25.6%
Congressional District 3	$32,500	$45,000	72.3%	27.7%
Congressional District 4	$34,900	$46,300	75.4%	24.6%
Congressional District 5	$43,000	$57,300	75.0%	25.0%
Congressional District 6	$34,000	$45,100	75.4%	24.6%
Congressional District 7	$33,700	$39,000	86.5%	13.5%
Congressional District 8	$31,800	$45,500	69.8%	30.2%
Congressional District 9	$35,000	$46,100	75.9%	24.1%
Iowa				
Congressional District 1	$35,400	$46,800	75.7%	24.3%
Congressional District 2	$36,300	$46,700	77.7%	22.3%
Congressional District 3	$41,100	$51,000	80.6%	19.4%
Congressional District 4	$32,800	$45,400	72.2%	27.8%
Kansas				
Congressional District 1	$31,400	$40,600	77.3%	22.7%
Congressional District 2	$35,700	$45,600	78.1%	21.9%
Congressional District 3	$41,600	$56,900	73.2%	26.8%
Congressional District 4	$35,300	$48,300	73.1%	26.9%
Kentucky				
Congressional District 1	$30,900	$40,400	76.4%	23.6%
Congressional District 2	$31,700	$41,200	77.1%	22.9%
Congressional District 3	$38,500	$45,400	84.8%	15.2%
Congressional District 4	$36,900	$50,000	73.8%	26.2%
Congressional District 5	$27,700	$37,300	74.3%	25.7%
Congressional District 6	$36,000	$41,900	85.7%	14.3%
Louisiana				
Congressional District 1	$36,300	$51,200	70.9%	29.1%
Congressional District 2	$31,200	$41,000	76.2%	23.8%
Congressional District 3	$30,700	$50,300	61.0%	39.0%
Congressional District 4	$30,100	$45,800	65.7%	34.3%
Congressional District 5	$27,400	$42,100	65.1%	34.9%
Congressional District 6	$35,700	$57,000	62.6%	37.4%
Maine				
Congressional District 1	$38,900	$49,800	78.2%	21.8%
Congressional District 2	$32,900	$41,900	78.4%	21.6%

Appendix Table: Gender Pay Gap by Congressional District (114th Congress)

Congressional District	Women's Median Earnings	Men's Median Earnings	Gender Earnings Ratio	Gender Pay Gap
Maryland				
Congressional District 1	$42,900	$55,500	77.4%	22.6%
Congressional District 2	$47,300	$51,300	92.2%	7.8%
Congressional District 3	$51,600	$62,000	83.2%	16.8%
Congressional District 4	$51,100	$51,400	99.3%	0.7%
Congressional District 5	$55,200	$61,000	90.5%	9.5%
Congressional District 6	$50,800	$60,000	84.7%	15.3%
Congressional District 7	$45,200	$57,500	78.6%	21.4%
Congressional District 8	$60,200	$74,400	81.0%	19.0%
Massachusetts				
Congressional District 1	$41,300	$50,800	81.3%	18.7%
Congressional District 2	$46,200	$56,900	81.2%	18.8%
Congressional District 3	$50,000	$62,100	80.5%	19.5%
Congressional District 4	$57,400	$72,200	79.5%	20.5%
Congressional District 5	$56,100	$70,200	79.9%	20.1%
Congressional District 6	$52,600	$68,200	77.1%	22.9%
Congressional District 7	$47,300	$52,100	90.8%	9.2%
Congressional District 8	$52,300	$66,200	79.0%	21.0%
Congressional District 9	$44,900	$58,700	76.4%	23.6%
Michigan				
Congressional District 1	$31,500	$42,500	74.2%	25.8%
Congressional District 2	$35,500	$45,900	77.3%	22.7%
Congressional District 3	$37,400	$47,300	79.1%	20.9%
Congressional District 4	$35,100	$45,100	78.0%	22.0%
Congressional District 5	$34,200	$45,400	75.3%	24.7%
Congressional District 6	$35,100	$44,800	78.3%	21.7%
Congressional District 7	$37,200	$49,500	75.1%	24.9%
Congressional District 8	$43,200	$61,500	70.3%	29.7%
Congressional District 9	$40,100	$51,300	78.1%	21.9%
Congressional District 10	$40,800	$53,600	76.2%	23.8%
Congressional District 11	$51,500	$70,100	73.4%	26.6%
Congressional District 12	$40,100	$51,800	77.3%	22.7%
Congressional District 13	$31,300	$40,000	78.2%	21.8%
Congressional District 14	$36,700	$47,400	77.5%	22.5%
Minnesota				
Congressional District 1	$37,300	$47,100	79.2%	20.8%
Congressional District 2	$46,700	$59,300	78.7%	21.3%
Congressional District 3	$50,600	$65,300	77.6%	22.4%
Congressional District 4	$46,800	$53,100	88.1%	11.9%
Congressional District 5	$45,800	$50,000	91.7%	8.3%
Congressional District 6	$42,500	$53,500	79.6%	20.4%

Appendix Table: Gender Pay Gap by Congressional District (114th Congress)

Congressional District	Women's Median Earnings	Men's Median Earnings	Gender Earnings Ratio	Gender Pay Gap
Minnesota (continued)				
Congressional District 7	$33,300	$43,700	76.2%	23.8%
Congressional District 8	$36,900	$49,200	75.2%	24.8%
Mississippi				
Congressional District 1	$31,800	$40,300	78.8%	21.2%
Congressional District 2	$29,100	$36,900	79.0%	21.0%
Congressional District 3	$33,200	$44,300	75.1%	24.9%
Congressional District 4	$31,300	$41,800	75.0%	25.0%
Missouri				
Congressional District 1	$35,800	$42,700	83.8%	16.2%
Congressional District 2	$45,900	$66,900	68.7%	31.3%
Congressional District 3	$36,900	$48,300	76.4%	23.6%
Congressional District 4	$31,900	$40,600	78.6%	21.4%
Congressional District 5	$35,200	$42,900	81.9%	18.1%
Congressional District 6	$36,100	$47,700	75.7%	24.3%
Congressional District 7	$30,900	$39,500	78.1%	21.9%
Congressional District 8	$29,700	$40,500	73.4%	26.6%
Montana				
Congressional District (at Large)	$31,700	$42,700	74.3%	25.7%
Nebraska				
Congressional District 1	$34,400	$44,900	76.5%	23.5%
Congressional District 2	$39,600	$47,400	83.6%	16.4%
Congressional District 3	$31,000	$41,300	75.1%	24.9%
Nevada				
Congressional District 1	$30,800	$33,200	92.8%	7.2%
Congressional District 2	$37,400	$46,500	80.3%	19.7%
Congressional District 3	$40,900	$51,300	79.7%	20.3%
Congressional District 4	$35,200	$42,100	83.6%	16.4%
New Hampshire				
Congressional District 1	$43,600	$56,800	76.9%	23.1%
Congressional District 2	$41,200	$54,300	75.9%	24.1%
New Jersey				
Congressional District 1	$45,500	$55,600	81.8%	18.2%
Congressional District 2	$40,500	$51,200	79.2%	20.8%
Congressional District 3	$50,000	$63,000	79.3%	20.7%
Congressional District 4	$50,700	$70,800	71.6%	28.4%
Congressional District 5	$52,100	$70,900	73.5%	26.5%
Congressional District 6	$48,900	$61,400	79.6%	20.4%
Congressional District 7	$61,800	$85,600	72.2%	27.8%
Congressional District 8	$40,800	$45,500	89.7%	10.3%
Congressional District 9	$41,700	$50,100	83.3%	16.7%

Appendix Table: Gender Pay Gap by Congressional District (114th Congress)

Congressional District	Women's Median Earnings	Men's Median Earnings	Gender Earnings Ratio	Gender Pay Gap
New Jersey (continued)				
Congressional District 10	$41,200	$47,900	86.0%	14.0%
Congressional District 11	$59,300	$80,800	73.4%	26.6%
Congressional District 12	$52,200	$62,200	83.9%	16.1%
New Mexico				
Congressional District 1	$35,900	$42,100	85.1%	14.9%
Congressional District 2	$29,500	$40,600	72.6%	27.4%
Congressional District 3	$34,700	$41,700	83.2%	16.8%
New York				
Congressional District 1	$50,900	$68,500	74.3%	25.7%
Congressional District 2	$47,200	$59,000	80.0%	20.0%
Congressional District 3	$60,900	$80,500	75.6%	24.4%
Congressional District 4	$54,000	$65,000	83.0%	17.0%
Congressional District 5	$41,900	$42,000	99.7%	0.3%
Congressional District 6	$45,900	$48,300	95.0%	5.0%
Congressional District 7	$41,700	$41,900	99.5%	0.5%
Congressional District 8	$41,300	$46,900	88.1%	11.9%
Congressional District 9	$41,900	$50,900	82.4%	17.6%
Congressional District 10	$68,000	$86,100	78.9%	21.1%
Congressional District 11	$47,900	$59,400	80.7%	19.3%
Congressional District 12	$74,300	$91,500	81.2%	18.8%
Congressional District 13	$39,800	$38,000	104.7%	-4.7%
Congressional District 14	$40,100	$37,100	108.0%	-8.0%
Congressional District 15	$28,800	$27,500	104.5%	-4.5%
Congressional District 16	$49,400	$56,700	87.1%	12.9%
Congressional District 17	$56,500	$71,400	79.2%	20.8%
Congressional District 18	$49,400	$61,100	80.8%	19.2%
Congressional District 19	$40,200	$50,000	80.4%	19.6%
Congressional District 20	$45,000	$52,500	85.8%	14.2%
Congressional District 21	$36,600	$45,600	80.4%	19.6%
Congressional District 22	$36,100	$45,000	80.2%	19.8%
Congressional District 23	$35,500	$42,800	82.8%	17.2%
Congressional District 24	$39,600	$48,800	81.1%	18.9%
Congressional District 25	$40,800	$48,600	84.0%	16.0%
Congressional District 26	$37,400	$45,100	83.0%	17.0%
Congressional District 27	$39,400	$50,900	77.5%	22.5%
North Carolina				
Congressional District 1	$31,700	$36,100	87.9%	12.1%
Congressional District 2	$35,000	$44,700	78.4%	21.6%
Congressional District 3	$33,800	$36,900	91.6%	8.4%
Congressional District 4	$37,500	$41,700	89.9%	10.1%

Appendix Table: Gender Pay Gap by Congressional District (114th Congress)

Congressional District	Women's Median Earnings	Men's Median Earnings	Gender Earnings Ratio	Gender Pay Gap
North Carolina (continued)				
Congressional District 5	$32,100	$41,400	77.5%	22.5%
Congressional District 6	$37,400	$44,700	83.6%	16.4%
Congressional District 7	$33,800	$40,800	83.0%	17.0%
Congressional District 8	$32,400	$40,900	79.4%	20.6%
Congressional District 9	$46,300	$61,900	74.8%	25.2%
Congressional District 10	$32,300	$39,900	81.1%	18.9%
Congressional District 11	$31,800	$37,000	85.9%	14.1%
Congressional District 12	$32,300	$36,100	89.6%	10.4%
Congressional District 13	$41,800	$52,800	79.1%	20.9%
North Dakota				
Congressional District (at Large)	$36,100	$50,600	71.3%	28.7%
Ohio				
Congressional District 1	$41,200	$51,400	80.1%	19.9%
Congressional District 2	$40,800	$50,100	81.5%	18.5%
Congressional District 3	$36,700	$40,500	90.6%	9.4%
Congressional District 4	$32,000	$45,500	70.3%	29.7%
Congressional District 5	$36,200	$48,700	74.4%	25.6%
Congressional District 6	$31,500	$42,400	74.3%	25.7%
Congressional District 7	$32,400	$44,000	73.7%	26.3%
Congressional District 8	$36,600	$47,100	77.7%	22.3%
Congressional District 9	$34,500	$43,300	79.8%	20.2%
Congressional District 10	$37,300	$48,800	76.5%	23.5%
Congressional District 11	$35,500	$44,100	80.5%	19.5%
Congressional District 12	$45,700	$58,900	77.6%	22.4%
Congressional District 13	$31,900	$43,100	74.1%	25.9%
Congressional District 14	$41,500	$55,700	74.4%	25.6%
Congressional District 15	$40,900	$50,700	80.5%	19.5%
Congressional District 16	$40,700	$52,500	77.5%	22.5%
Oklahoma				
Congressional District 1	$35,200	$46,100	76.4%	23.6%
Congressional District 2	$30,000	$39,700	75.5%	24.5%
Congressional District 3	$31,500	$45,800	68.7%	31.3%
Congressional District 4	$32,500	$45,900	70.8%	29.2%
Congressional District 5	$33,600	$42,100	79.8%	20.2%
Oregon				
Congressional District 1	$42,700	$57,400	74.4%	25.6%
Congressional District 2	$32,700	$40,900	79.9%	20.1%
Congressional District 3	$41,900	$47,400	88.4%	11.6%
Congressional District 4	$36,000	$43,700	82.4%	17.6%
Congressional District 5	$37,300	$46,500	80.2%	19.8%

Appendix Table: Gender Pay Gap by Congressional District (114th Congress)

Congressional District	Women's Median Earnings	Men's Median Earnings	Gender Earnings Ratio	Gender Pay Gap
Pennsylvania				
Congressional District 1	$40,600	$42,200	96.3%	3.7%
Congressional District 2	$41,200	$48,900	84.3%	15.7%
Congressional District 3	$35,300	$46,400	76.1%	23.9%
Congressional District 4	$38,400	$50,100	76.7%	23.3%
Congressional District 5	$33,600	$44,600	75.4%	24.6%
Congressional District 6	$46,600	$61,000	76.4%	23.6%
Congressional District 7	$48,600	$64,900	74.8%	25.2%
Congressional District 8	$49,500	$61,900	79.9%	20.1%
Congressional District 9	$31,900	$42,500	75.0%	25.0%
Congressional District 10	$32,900	$44,200	74.6%	25.4%
Congressional District 11	$36,200	$46,600	77.8%	22.2%
Congressional District 12	$40,600	$51,900	78.2%	21.8%
Congressional District 13	$45,600	$50,800	89.7%	10.3%
Congressional District 14	$38,100	$45,000	84.8%	15.2%
Congressional District 15	$37,700	$50,700	74.4%	25.6%
Congressional District 16	$36,700	$48,600	75.6%	24.4%
Congressional District 17	$36,200	$45,700	79.2%	20.8%
Congressional District 18	$41,700	$56,900	73.4%	26.6%
Puerto Rico				
Resident Commissioner	$22,900	$21,900	104.8%	-4.8%
Rhode Island				
Congressional District 1	$41,300	$50,300	82.1%	17.9%
Congressional District 2	$41,700	$51,300	81.3%	18.7%
South Carolina				
Congressional District 1	$39,100	$48,400	80.9%	19.1%
Congressional District 2	$37,600	$47,000	80.0%	20.0%
Congressional District 3	$31,700	$41,100	77.2%	22.8%
Congressional District 4	$34,400	$42,500	81.1%	18.9%
Congressional District 5	$32,700	$42,500	77.0%	23.0%
Congressional District 6	$29,900	$32,100	93.0%	7.0%
Congressional District 7	$30,900	$39,700	77.7%	22.3%
South Dakota				
Congressional District (at Large)	$32,000	$42,000	76.2%	23.8%
Tennessee				
Congressional District 1	$29,400	$36,900	79.7%	20.3%
Congressional District 2	$35,400	$43,500	81.4%	18.6%
Congressional District 3	$32,900	$41,700	78.9%	21.1%
Congressional District 4	$32,500	$42,000	77.5%	22.5%
Congressional District 5	$37,200	$41,200	90.4%	9.6%
Congressional District 6	$32,900	$41,600	79.0%	21.0%

Appendix Table: Gender Pay Gap by Congressional District (114th Congress)

Congressional District	Women's Median Earnings	Men's Median Earnings	Gender Earnings Ratio	Gender Pay Gap
Tennessee (continued)				
Congressional District 7	$35,100	$47,000	74.7%	25.3%
Congressional District 8	$36,900	$49,000	75.4%	24.6%
Congressional District 9	$33,100	$33,000	100.2%	-0.2%
Texas				
Congressional District 1	$32,000	$41,900	76.3%	23.7%
Congressional District 2	$46,600	$57,200	81.5%	18.5%
Congressional District 3	$51,500	$72,400	71.1%	28.9%
Congressional District 4	$31,800	$43,700	72.7%	27.3%
Congressional District 5	$32,300	$38,100	84.9%	15.1%
Congressional District 6	$39,200	$50,000	78.4%	21.6%
Congressional District 7	$46,100	$60,900	75.7%	24.3%
Congressional District 8	$37,600	$54,000	69.7%	30.3%
Congressional District 9	$31,900	$32,400	98.2%	1.8%
Congressional District 10	$43,000	$54,900	78.4%	21.6%
Congressional District 11	$30,900	$50,900	60.7%	39.3%
Congressional District 12	$40,900	$50,800	80.4%	19.6%
Congressional District 13	$30,600	$44,600	68.6%	31.4%
Congressional District 14	$37,500	$51,000	73.4%	26.6%
Congressional District 15	$30,600	$36,700	83.3%	16.7%
Congressional District 16	$29,600	$36,500	80.9%	19.1%
Congressional District 17	$34,400	$44,500	77.4%	22.6%
Congressional District 18	$32,200	$38,600	83.4%	16.6%
Congressional District 19	$30,400	$40,900	74.4%	25.6%
Congressional District 20	$33,400	$37,200	89.8%	10.2%
Congressional District 21	$42,200	$52,100	81.0%	19.0%
Congressional District 22	$50,100	$71,800	69.9%	30.1%
Congressional District 23	$30,100	$45,200	66.5%	33.5%
Congressional District 24	$44,900	$55,200	81.3%	18.7%
Congressional District 25	$40,300	$50,100	80.5%	19.5%
Congressional District 26	$47,700	$60,900	78.2%	21.8%
Congressional District 27	$30,900	$45,300	68.2%	31.8%
Congressional District 28	$30,500	$39,100	77.9%	22.1%
Congressional District 29	$26,800	$32,400	82.6%	17.4%
Congressional District 30	$33,500	$36,900	90.7%	9.3%
Congressional District 31	$39,300	$49,500	79.6%	20.4%
Congressional District 32	$45,500	$51,200	88.8%	11.2%
Congressional District 33	$25,800	$29,200	88.5%	11.5%
Congressional District 34	$26,700	$34,600	77.4%	22.6%
Congressional District 35	$30,400	$34,600	88.0%	12.0%
Congressional District 36	$35,300	$52,200	67.6%	32.4%
Utah				
Congressional District 1	$34,900	$51,600	67.7%	32.3%
Congressional District 2	$31,900	$45,800	69.6%	30.4%
Congressional District 3	$36,400	$57,300	63.6%	36.4%
Congressional District 4	$33,300	$50,200	66.4%	33.6%

Appendix Table: Gender Pay Gap by Congressional District (114th Congress)

Congressional District	Women's Median Earnings	Men's Median Earnings	Gender Earnings Ratio	Gender Pay Gap
Vermont				
Congressional District (at Large)	$39,300	$46,900	83.8%	16.2%
Virginia				
Congressional District 1	$43,400	$60,400	71.8%	28.2%
Congressional District 2	$36,900	$46,200	79.8%	20.2%
Congressional District 3	$33,700	$39,100	86.2%	13.8%
Congressional District 4	$39,300	$50,800	77.3%	22.7%
Congressional District 5	$35,900	$45,300	79.3%	20.7%
Congressional District 6	$35,400	$43,200	81.9%	18.1%
Congressional District 7	$45,900	$57,700	79.5%	20.5%
Congressional District 8	$65,600	$76,300	86.0%	14.0%
Congressional District 9	$33,200	$42,000	79.0%	21.0%
Congressional District 10	$59,100	$87,200	67.7%	32.3%
Congressional District 11	$58,500	$70,000	83.6%	16.4%
Washington				
Congressional District 1	$46,900	$72,400	64.7%	35.3%
Congressional District 2	$41,400	$51,400	80.7%	19.3%
Congressional District 3	$37,900	$51,300	73.9%	26.1%
Congressional District 4	$32,300	$41,900	77.1%	22.9%
Congressional District 5	$36,700	$46,600	78.8%	21.2%
Congressional District 6	$40,400	$51,000	79.2%	20.8%
Congressional District 7	$51,900	$67,300	77.0%	23.0%
Congressional District 8	$46,000	$61,600	74.7%	25.3%
Congressional District 9	$45,600	$56,800	80.3%	19.7%
Congressional District 10	$40,600	$49,700	81.7%	18.3%
West Virginia				
Congressional District 1	$32,100	$43,900	73.2%	26.8%
Congressional District 2	$34,500	$45,900	75.2%	24.8%
Congressional District 3	$28,700	$45,000	63.8%	36.2%
Wisconsin				
Congressional District 1	$39,900	$51,600	77.3%	22.7%
Congressional District 2	$41,700	$50,600	82.5%	17.5%
Congressional District 3	$34,700	$42,600	81.5%	18.5%
Congressional District 4	$35,900	$41,600	86.3%	13.7%
Congressional District 5	$42,700	$55,500	77.0%	23.0%
Congressional District 6	$35,700	$47,200	75.8%	24.2%
Congressional District 7	$35,800	$44,600	80.4%	19.6%
Congressional District 8	$36,800	$47,000	78.3%	21.7%
Wyoming				
Congressional District (at Large)	$35,700	$51,900	68.7%	31.3%

Source: JEC Democratic staff calculations based on data from the U.S. Census Bureau, 2014 American Community Survey (1-year estimates) using American FactFinder

Notes: Data are based on median annual earnings of those who have worked full time, year-round in the past 12 months; earnings data are in 2014 inflation-adjusted dollars, rounded to nearest hundred dollars; population 16 years and over with earnings

SOURCES

[1] According to the U.S. Equal Employment Opportunity Commission (EEOC), "The Equal Pay Act requires that men and women in the same workplace be given equal pay for equal work. The jobs need not be identical, but they must be substantially equal. Job content (not job titles) determines whether jobs are substantially equal. All forms of pay are covered by this law, including salary, overtime pay, bonuses, stock options, profit sharing and bonus plans, life insurance, vacation and holiday pay, cleaning or gasoline allowances, hotel accommodations, reimbursement for travel expenses, and benefits. If there is an inequality in wages between men and women, employers may not reduce the wages of either sex to equalize their pay."

[2] EEOC, "Title VII of the Civil Rights Act of 1964"; and Benjamin Collins and Jody Feder, "Pay Equity: Legislative and Legal Developments" Congressional Research Service (November 22, 2013).

[3] U.S. Census Bureau, Historical Income Tables Table P-40: Women's Earnings as a Percentage of Men's Earnings by Race and Hispanic Origin (Data for 2014 are the most recent available and are based on median earnings of full-time, year-round workers 15 and older as of March 2015).

[4] According to the Center for American Progress, the "career earnings gap" is now nearly $434,000. The Institute for Women's Policy Research (IWPR) has separately estimated that women born between 1955 and 1959 who worked full time, year-round each year lost more than $530,000 by the time they reached age 59.

[5] IWPR, "Women Will Not See Equal Pay with Men until 2059, One Year Longer than Previously Projected" (September 2015).

[6] Child Care Aware of America, "Parents and the High Cost of Child Care, 2015" (December 2015).

[7] JEC Democratic Staff 114th Congress, "How Working Mothers Contribute to the Economic Security of American Families" (May 7, 2015).

[8] Francine D. Blau and Lawrence M. Kahn, "The Gender Pay Gap: Have Women Gone as Far as They Can?" *Academy of Management Perspectives*, vol. 21, no. 1 (2007) pp. 7-23.

[9] Bureau of Labor Statistics, Current Population Survey, Table 3. Employment status of the civilian noninstitutional population by age, sex, and race (2014 annual averages); and Bureau of Labor Statistics, Current Employment Statistics, Table B-5. Employment of women on nonfarm payrolls by industry sector, seasonally adjusted (as of January 8, 2016).

[10] U.S. Census Bureau, Historical Income Tables Table P-40: Women's Earnings as a Percentage of Men's Earnings by Race and Hispanic Origin; Based on annual data from the U.S. Census Bureau's 2014 American Community Survey (Table S2002), women's median annual earnings were 79.9 percent of men's. This estimate is also based on data for full-time, year-round workers.

[11] U.S. Census Bureau, Historical Income Tables Table P-40: Women's Earnings as a Percentage of Men's Earnings by Race and Hispanic Origin (September 2015).

[12] Economic Policy Institute (EPI), "EPI Announces Bold Agenda to Raise Women's Wages" (November 18, 2015). According to EPI, 40 percent of the closing of the gender wage gap over the last 35 years was due to men's declining wages.

[13] JEC Democratic staff calculations based on data from the U.S. Census Bureau, Historical Income Tables Table P-8. Age—People, All Races, by Median Income and Sex: 1947 to 2014 (September 2015).

[14] National Women's Law Center, "The Wage Gap: The Who, How, Why and What to Do" (April 1, 2016).

[15] IWPR, "Status of Women in the States: 2015" (May 2015) Figure 2.5. According to calculations by IWPR, women born between 1955 and 1959 who worked full time, year-round each year lost an average of $531,502 by age 59. The losses were even greater for college-educated women (nearly $800,000). That is based on the difference between the median annual earnings of women and men who worked full time, year-round each year.

[16] These estimates are from fact sheets recently released by the National Women's Law Center on the lifetime wage gap for African-American, Hispanic, Asian-American and Native-American women.

[17] IWPR, "Status of Women in the States: 2015" (May 2015) Figure 2.5

[18] Women's Institute for a Secure Retirement (WISER), "and...The Pay Gap's Connected to the Retirement Gap!" (2015).

[19] JEC Democratic staff calculations based on data from the U.S. Census Bureau, PINC-08: Source of Income in 2014 - People 15 Years Old and Over, by Income of Specified Type in 2014, Age, Race, Hispanic Origin, and Sex (Both Sexes, 65 Years and Over, All Races).

[20] Ibid.

[21] U.S. Census Bureau, PINC-01. Selected Characteristics of People 15 Years and Over, by Total Money Income in 2014, Work Experience in 2014, Race, Hispanic Origin, and Sex (Total Work Experience, All Races for Males and Females).

[22] Bureau of Labor Statistics, Labor Force Participation Rate – 65 years and over, women.

[23] JEC Democratic staff calculations based on data from the U.S. Census Bureau, PINC-08: Source of Income in 2014 - People 15 Years Old and Over, by Income of Specified Type in 2014, Age, Race, Hispanic Origin, and Sex (Female, 65 Years and Over, All Races).

[24] Jennifer Erin Brown, M.S., J.D., LL.M. and Nari Rhee, Ph.D., "Shortchanged in Retirement: Continuing Challenges to Women's Financial Future" National Institute on Retirement Security (March 2016).

[25] Social Security Administration, Office of Retirement and Disability Policy, Income of the Population 55 or Older, 2012, Table 9.B1: Percentage distribution of persons in beneficiary families, by sex and age, 2012; and Jocelyn Fischer and Jeff Hayes, Ph.D., "The Importance of Social Security in the Incomes of Older Americans: Differences by Gender, Age, Race/Ethnicity, and Marital Status" (August 2013).

[26] National Partnership for Women & Families, "Social Security At A Glance" (accessed January 20, 2016).

[27] JEC Democratic staff calculations based on data from the Social Security Administration, Office of the Chief Actuary, Average monthly benefit for retired workers in December 2015, (accessed January 13, 2015). The average monthly retirement benefit among female beneficiaries was $1,182.36, compared with $1,500.46 for male beneficiaries.

[28] Mikki D. Waid, Ph.D., "An Uphill Climb: Women Face Greater Obstacles to Retirement Security" AARP Public Policy Institute (April 2013).

[29] Women's Institute for a Secure Retirement (WISER), "and...The Pay Gap's Connected to the Retirement Gap!" (2015).

[30] JEC Democratic staff calculations based on data from the U.S. Census Bureau, PINC-08: Source of Income in 2014 - People 15 Years Old and Over, by Income of Specified Type in 2014, Age, Race, Hispanic Origin, and Sex (Both Sexes, 65 Years and Over, All Races).

[31] Berhanu Alemayehu and Kenneth E. Warner, "The Lifetime Distribution of Health Care Costs" *Health Services Research,* vol. 39, no. 3 (June 2004) pp. 627-642.

[32] U.S. Census Bureau, Table POV01: Age and Sex of All People, Family Members and Unrelated Individuals Iterated by Income-to-Poverty Ratio and Race (Below 100 Percent of Poverty, All Races, 2014).

[33] JEC Democratic staff calculations based on data from U.S. Census Bureau, Current Population Survey, 2015 Annual Social and Economic Supplement (using CPS Table Creator); and Kathleen Romig, Center on Budget and Policy Priorities, "Social Security Lifts 21 Million Americans Out of Poverty" (November 9, 2015).

[34] U.S. Census Bureau, Table POV01: Age and Sex of All People, Family Members and Unrelated Individuals Iterated by Income-to-Poverty Ratio and Race (Below 100 Percent of Poverty, Black Alone, Asian Alone, Hispanic (any race), 2014).

[35] While less significant than other factors, studies have found that race can affect the gender pay gap. Specifically, Francine Blau and Laurence Kahn estimated two percent of the gap is attributable to race. For additional discussion, see Francine D. Blau and Lawrence M. Kahn, "The Gender Pay Gap: Have Women Gone as Far as They Can?" *Academy of Management Perspectives*, vol. 21, no. 1 (2007) pp. 7-23.

[36] JEC Democratic staff calculations based on data from U.S. Census Bureau, Current Population Survey 2015 Annual Social and Economic Supplement. Historical Income Tables Table P-41. Work Experience — Workers by Median Earnings and Sex: 1987 to 2014 (September 2015). "White" refers to "White Alone, not Hispanic"; dollars are rounded to nearest hundred; full-time, year-round workers include those who work 50 to 52 weeks on a full-time basis.

[37] JEC Democratic staff calculations based on data from U.S. Census Bureau, Current Population Survey 2015 Annual Social and Economic Supplement. Historical Income Tables Table P-41. Work Experience — Workers by Median Earnings and Sex: 1987 to 2014 (September 2015). "Black" refers to "Black Alone or in Combination"; "Hispanic" refers to "Hispanic (any race)"; "Asian" refers to "Asian Alone"; dollars are rounded to nearest hundred; full-time, year-round workers include those who work 50 to 52 weeks on a full-time basis.

[38] Comparisons between racial and ethnic groups are calculated based on data from the U.S. Census Bureau, Current Population Survey 2015 Annual Social and Economic Supplement. Historical Income Tables Table P-41. Work Experience—Workers by Median Earnings and Sex. "White" refers to "White Alone, not Hispanic"; "Black" refers to "Black Alone or in Combination"; "Hispanic" refers to "Hispanic (any race)"; "Asian" refers to "Asian Alone"; dollars are rounded to nearest hundred; full-time, year-round workers include those who work 50 to 52 weeks on a full-time basis.

[39] JEC Democratic staff calculations based on data from U.S. Census Bureau, 2014 American Community Survey 1-year estimates. Tables B24010H, B24010B, B24010I, B24010D and S2410. For additional discussion, see Liana Christin Landivar, "Disparities in STEM Employment by Sex, Race, and Hispanic Origin" U.S. Census Bureau American Community Survey Reports (Issued September 2013).

[40] Ibid.

[41] Milia Fisher, "Women of Color and the Gender Wage Gap" Center for American Progress (April 14, 2015).

[42] Rachel O'Connor, Jeff Hayes, Ph.D. and Barbara Gault, Ph.D., Fact Sheet: Paid Sick Days Access Varies by Race/Ethnicity, Sexual Orientation, and Job Characteristics," IWPR (July 2014); Council of Economic Advisers, "The Economics of Paid and Unpaid Leave" (June 2014); and Milia Fisher, "Women of Color and the Gender Wage Gap" Center for American Progress (April 14, 2015).

[43] JEC Democratic staff calculations based on data from U.S. Census Bureau, Current Population Survey 2015 Annual Social and Economic Supplement.

[44] American Association of University Women, "The Simple Truth about the Gender Pay Gap, Spring 2016 Edition" (February 6, 2016), p. 12.

[45] JEC Democratic staff calculations based on data from U.S. Census Bureau, Current Population Survey 2015 Annual Social and Economic Supplement.

[46] Pew Research Center, "On Pay Gap, Millennial Women Near Parity – For Now," (December 11, 2013). The cited survey includes women who have ever been employed; percentages and information on statistical significance not appearing in the publication was provided directly by Pew Research Center staff.

[47] JEC Democratic staff calculations based on data from U.S. Census Bureau, Current Population Survey 2015 Annual Social and Economic Supplement.

[48] Michelle J. Budig and Paula England, "The Wage Penalty for Motherhood" American Sociological Review, vol. 66 (April 2001), pp. 204-225.

[49] For example, in "Getting a Job: Is There a Motherhood Penalty?" (March 2007), Shelley J. Correll, Stephen Benard, and In Paik found evidence of discrimination against mothers during the hiring process. They note that "consistent with theoretical predictions, competence and commitment to mediate, at least partially, the negative effect of motherhood status on workplace evaluations. In part, mothers are rated as less hirable, less suitable for promotion and management training, and deserving of lower salaries because they are believed to be less competent and less committed to paid work."

[50] Melissa Alpert and Alexandra Cawthorne, "Labor Pains: Improving Employment and Income Security for Pregnant Women and New Mothers" Center for American Progress (August 3, 2009).

[51] T.J. Mathews, M.S. and Brady E. Hamilton, Ph.D., "NCHS Data Brief: First Births to Older Women Continue to Rise" Centers for Disease Control and Prevention (May 2014); National Center for Health Statistics, National Vital Statistics Reports, "Births: Final Data for 2014" (December 23, 2015); and T.J. Mathews, M.S. and Brady E. Hamilton, Ph.D., "NCHS Data Brief: Delayed Childbearing: More Women Are Having Their First Child Later in Life" Centers for Disease Control and Prevention (August 2009).

[52] JEC Democratic staff calculations based on data from U.S. Census Bureau, Current Population Survey Annual Social and Economic Supplements (data for 1989 and 2014).

[53] JEC Democratic staff calculations based on data from U.S. Census Bureau 2014 American Community Survey, 1-year estimates.

[54] For additional discussion of state laws, see American Association of University Women, "The Simple Truth about the Gender Pay Gap, Spring 2016 Edition" (February 6, 2016), pp. 22-24.

[55] JEC Democratic staff calculations based on data from Bureau of Labor Statistics, Establishment Survey. Women's share of nonfarm payroll employment averaged 31.8 percent in 1964.

[56] Bureau of Labor Statistics, Labor Force Participation Rate – 25- to 54-years, women. The annual average in 1964 was 44.5 percent.

[57] U.S. Census Bureau, "Income in 1965 of Families and Persons in the United States" Table 2 (January 12, 1967).

[58] Council of Economic Advisers, "The Labor Force Participation Rate Since 2007: Causes and Policy Implications" (July 2014).

[59] JEC Democratic staff calculations based on data from Bureau of Labor Statistics, Unpublished Table: Employment status of the civilian noninstitutional population by sex, age, presence and age of youngest child, marital status, race, and Hispanic origin, March 2014 ASEC (provided on December 3, 2015); and Bureau of Labor Statistics, Unpublished Table: Wives who earn more than their husbands, 1987-2013. According to BLS, in 2013, among wives with earnings, 38.1 percent earned more than their husbands (who may not have had earnings) (provided on December 3, 2015).

[60] JEC Democratic staff calculations based on data from Bureau of Labor Statistics, Unpublished Table: Employment status of the civilian noninstitutional population by sex, age, presence and age of youngest child, marital status, race, and Hispanic origin, March 2014 ASEC (Provided on December 3, 2015).

[61] Council of Economic Advisers, "Nine Facts about American Families and Work" (June 2014).

[62] JEC Democratic staff calculations based on data from U.S. Census Bureau, American Community Survey 2014 1-year estimates. Table B23008. Calculation includes children who live with a single parent who is not in the labor force, and children in two-parent families where one or both parents are out of the labor force.

[63] JEC Democratic staff calculations based on data from the U.S. Census Bureau, Current Population Survey, 2015 Annual Social and Economic Supplement. In 2014, in families with a child under 18 years old, the median contribution to family income from working mothers was 38.0 percent.

[64] JEC Democratic staff calculations based on data from the U.S. Census Bureau, Current Population Survey, 2015 Annual Social and Economic Supplement.

[65] Heidi Hartmann, Ph.D., Jeffrey Hayes, Ph.D., and Jennifer Clark, "How Equal Pay for Working Women Would Reduce Poverty and Grow the American Economy" IWPR (January 2014).

[66] U.S. Department of Agriculture, "Expenditures on Children by Families, 2013" (August 2014).

[67] Ibid. The 2 percent of child-rearing expenditures on child care and education in 1960 includes families with and without the expense. The 18 percent is for families with the expense. The increased child care costs reflect the increase in women's participation in the labor force and the growing need for child care.

[68] U.S. Department of Agriculture, "Expenditures on Children by Families, 2013" (August 2014); Council of Economic Advisers, "Trends in Health Care Cost Growth and the Role of the Affordable Care Act" (November 2013). Ratio of health care inflation relative to general price inflation was 1.8 from 1965 until the Affordable Care Act.

[69] Mary Daly and Tali Regev, "Labor Force Participation and the Prospects for U.S. Growth" *FRBSF Economic Letter*, Federal Reserve Bank of San Francisco (November 2, 2007).

[70] Council of Economic Advisers, *Economic Report of the President* (February 2016).

[71] Testimony of Dr. Elisabeth S. Jacobs, Senior Director for Policy and Academic Programs, Washington Center for Equitable Growth, before the U.S. Congress Joint Economic Committee, "The Declining Labor Force Participation Rate: Causes, Consequences, and the Path Forward" (July 15, 2015).

[72] Council of Economic Advisers "2015 Economic Report of the President" (February 2015).

[73] Christine Lagarde, "Dare the Difference" International Monetary Fund *Finance and Development*, vol. 50, no. 2 (June 2013).

[74] Heidi Hartmann, Ph.D., Jeffrey Hayes, Ph.D., and Jennifer Clark, "How Equal Pay for Working Women Would Reduce Poverty and Grow the American Economy" IWPR (January 2014).

[75] Organisation for Economic Co-operation and Development (OECD), "Closing the Gender Gap: Act Now" Table I.A3.1 (December 17, 2012).

[76] OECD, "In It Together: Why Less Inequality Benefits All" (May 21, 2015).

[77] Kim Parker, "Despite progress, women still bear heavier load than men in balancing work and family" Pew Research Center (March 10, 2015).

[78] American Association of University Women, "The Simple Truth about the Gender Pay Gap, Spring 2016 Edition" (February 6, 2016), p. 9.

[79] JEC Democratic staff calculations based on data from Bureau of Labor Statistics, Unpublished Table: Employment status of the civilian noninstitutional population by sex, age, presence and age of youngest child, marital status, race, and Hispanic origin, March 2014 ASEC (Provided on December 3, 2015).

[80] Lynda Laughlin, "Maternity Leave and Employment Patters of First-Time Mothers, 1961-2008" U.S. Census Bureau (October 2011).

[81] Eileen Patten, "On Equal Pay Day, key facts about the gender pay gap" Pew Research Center (April 14, 2015).

[82] Pew Research Center, "2015 Survey of American Parents Final Topline, September 15-October 13, 2015" (November 4, 2015).

[83] Catalyst, "Women Leaving and Re-Entering the Workforce" (March 28, 2013).

[84] Jane Waldfogel, "Understanding the 'Family Gap' in Pay for Women with Children" *The Journal of Economic Perspectives*, vol. 12, no. 1 (Winter 1998) pp. 137-156; Barbara Gault, Ph.D., Heidi Hartmann, Ph.D., Ariane Hegewisch, Jessica Milli, Ph.D., and Lindsey Reichlin, M.A. "Paid Parental Leave in the United States: What the Data Tell Us about Access, Usage, and Economic and Health Benefits" IWPR (January 2014); and Heather Boushey, Ann O'Leary and Alexandra Mitukiewicz, "The Economic Benefits of Family and Medical Leave Insurance" Center for American Progress (December 12, 2013).

[85] Human Impact Partners, "Fact Sheet: Parental Leave and the Health of Infants, Children and Mothers" (November 2011).

[86] JEC Democratic staff calculations based on data from the U.S. Census Bureau, Current Population Survey (annual average of monthly Microdata files).

[87] Michelle J. Budig, Ph.D., "The Fatherhood Bonus and the Motherhood Penalty: Parenthood and the Gender Gap in Pay" (September 2, 2014).

[88] Kim Parker, "Despite progress, women still bear heavier load than men in balancing work and family" Pew Research Center (March 10, 2015).

[89] Council of Economic Advisers "2015 Economic Report of the President" Chapter 4: The Economics of Family-Friendly Workplace Policies, Table 4-4: Access to Leave and Workplace Flexibility by Demographic, Educational, and Worker

Characteristics, 2011 (February 2015); and Ann Bartel, Maya Rossin-Slater, Christopher Ruhm, Jenna Stearns and Jane Waldfogel, "Paid Family Leave, Fathers' Leave-Taking, and Leave-Sharing in Duel-Earner Households" National Bureau of Economic Research (November 2015); Claire Cain Miller, "Paternity Leave: The Rewards and the Remaining Stigma" *The New York Times* (November 7, 2014).

[90] Eileen Patten, "On Equal Pay Day, key facts about the gender pay gap" Pew Research Center (April 14, 2015).

[91] AARP Public Policy Institute and National Alliance for Caregiving, "Caregiving in the U.S. 2015" (June 2015).

[92] MetLife, "The MetLife Study of Caregiving Costs to Working Caregivers: Double Jeopardy for Baby Boomers Caring for Their Parents" (June 2011).

[93] For example, according to "Why U.S. Women Are Leaving Jobs Behind" *The New York Times* (December 12, 2014), "In a New York Times/CBS News/Kaiser Family Foundation poll of nonworking adults aged 25 to 54 in the United States, conducted last month, 61 percent of women said family responsibilities were a reason they weren't working, compared with 37 percent of men. Of women who identify as homemakers and have not looked for a job in the last year, nearly three-quarters said they would consider going back if a job offered flexible hours or allowed them to work from home."

[94] JEC Democratic staff calculations based on data from the Bureau of Labor Statistics, Table 8. Employed and unemployed full- and part-time workers by age, sex, race and Hispanic or Latino ethnicity, Household data, annual averages (2014 annual averages).

[95] JEC Democratic Staff 111th Congress, "The Earnings Penalty for Part-Time Work: An Obstacle to Equal Pay" (April 20, 2010).

[96] JEC Democratic Staff 111th Congress, "The Earnings Penalty for Part-Time Work: An Obstacle to Equal Pay" (April 20, 2010).

[97] JEC Democratic staff calculations based on data from National Center for Education Statistics, Table 318.30. Bachelor's, master's, and doctor's degrees conferred by postsecondary institutions, by sex of student and discipline division: 2012-13.

[98] Blau and Kahn found that the greater educational attainment among women employed full time helped to narrow the gender wage gap. See Francine D. Blau and Lawrence M. Kahn, "The Gender Pay Gap: Have Women Gone as Far as They Can?" *Academy of Management Perspectives*, vol. 21, no. 1 (2007) pp. 7-23.

[99] IWPR, "Status of Women in the States: 2015" (May 2015) Figure 2.4.

[100] IWPR, "Status of Women in the States: 2015" (May 2015) Figure 2.4.

[101] National Center for Education Statistics, "Fast Facts: Degrees Conferred by Sex and Race"; Julie Siebens and Camille L. Ryan, "Field of Bachelor's Degree in the United States: 2009" U.S. Census Bureau (February 2012); and Christianne Corbett, M.A. and Catherine Hill, Ph.D., "Graduating to a Pay Gap: The Earnings of Women and Men One Year after College Graduation" American Association of University Women (October 2012).

[102] JEC Democratic staff calculations based on data from the U.S. Census Bureau 2014 American Community Survey 1-year estimates Table B15011. More than half (51.8 percent) of 25- to 39-year olds with a college degree in science or engineering are women, compared with nearly 46 percent of 40- to 64-year olds. Calculations include "science and engineering" and "science and engineering related" categories.

[103] JEC Democratic staff calculations based on data from National Center for Education Statistics, Table 318.30. Bachelor's, master's, and doctor's degrees conferred by postsecondary institutions, by sex of student and discipline division: 2012-13; and Georgetown Center on Education and the Workforce, "The Economic Value of College Majors" (2015).

[104] Ibid.

[105] Ariane Hegewisch, Heidi Hartmann, Ph.D., "Occupational Segregation and the Gender Wage Gap: A Job Half Done" IWPR (January 2014).

[106] Samantha Nix, Lara Perez-Felkner and Kirby Thomas, "Perceived mathematical ability under challenge: a longitudinal perspective on sex segregation among STEM degree fields" *Frontiers in Psychology,* vol.6, no. 530 (June 9, 2015) pp. 1-19.

[107] For examples, see Elena Weissmann, "Female STEM students cite isolation, lack of role models" *The Brown Daily Herald* (April 23, 2015); Laura Bonetta, "Reaching Gender Equity in Science: The Importance of Role Models and Mentors" *Science* (February 12, 2010); and Balaji Ganapathy et al., "Women in STEM: Realizing the Potential" STEMconnector (March 2014).

[108] JEC Democratic staff calculations based on data from Bureau of Labor Statistics, Table 39. Median weekly earnings of full-time wage and salary workers by detailed occupation and sex, 2014 annual averages data from the U.S. Census Bureau, Current Population Survey, 2014. Ibid. Comparing weekly earnings of full-time employees within occupations helps control for part-time or part-year work schedules. While the typical weekly hours may be different for men and women within the same occupations, estimates of median weekly earnings are based on only workers who worked at least 35 hours per week, as defined by the U.S. Census Bureau.

[109] Ariane, Hegewisch, Claudia Williams, and Vanessa Harbin, "The Gender Wage Gap by Occupation" Institute for Women's Policy Research (April 2012).

[110] U.S. Department of Labor Women's Bureau, "Most Common Occupations for Women."

[111] Nancy Folbre, "Why Girly Jobs Don't Pay Well" *The New York Times* (August 16, 2010).

[112] Ariane Hegewisch and Heidi Hartmann, Ph.D., "Occupational Segregation and the Gender Wage Gap: A Job Half Done" IWPR (January 2014).

[113] JEC Democratic staff calculations based on data from Bureau of Labor Statistics, Table 39. Median weekly earnings of full-time wage and salary workers by detailed occupation and sex, 2014 annual averages.

[114] Ariane Hegewisch, Claudia Williams, and Vanessa Harbin, "The Gender Wage Gap by Occupation" IWPR (April 2012).

[115] Bureau of Labor Statistics, Table 39. Median weekly earnings of full-time wage and salary workers by detailed occupation and sex, 2014 annual averages.

[116] Ibid.

[117] JEC Democratic staff calculations based on data from Bureau of Labor Statistics, Table 39. Median weekly earnings of full-time wage and salary workers by detailed occupation and sex, 2014 annual averages. Notably, median weekly earnings of men who worked as physicians or surgeons were $2,002, compared with median weekly earnings of $1,246 for women who worked as physicians or surgeons. Median weekly earnings of men who worked as registered nurses were $1,090, compared with median weekly earnings of $1,076 for women.

[118] JEC Democratic staff calculations based on data from Bureau of Labor Statistics, Table 39. Median weekly earnings of full-time wage and salary workers by detailed occupation and sex, 2014 annual averages.

[119] Bureau of Labor Statistics, Current Population Survey Table 11. Employed persons by detailed occupation, sex, race and Hispanic or Latino ethnicity (2014 annual averages).

[120] Testimony of Heather Boushey, Senior Economist, Center for American Progress, before the U.S. Senate Committee on Health, Education, Labor and Pensions, "Strengthening the Middle Class: Ensuring Equal Pay for Women" (March 11, 2010).

[121] James T. Bond and Ellen Galinsky "Workplace Flexibility and Low-Wage Employees" *Families and Work Institute National Study of the Changing Workforce* (2011) and Bureau of Labor Statistics, National Compensation Survey Table 46. Paid leave combinations: Access, civilian workers, March 2015.

[122] U.S. Census Bureau, "QuickFacts" (accessed January 20, 2016).

[123] Jennifer E. Manning, "Membership of the 114th Congress: A Profile" Congressional Research Service (December 1, 2015).

[124] Center for American Women and Politics (CAWP), "Women in Statewide Elective Executive Office 2015" Eagleton Institute of Politics, Rutgers, The State University of New Jersey; and CAWP, "Women in State Legislatures 2015" Eagleton Institute of Politics, Rutgers, The State University of New Jersey.

[125] CAWP, "Current Numbers" Eagleton Institute for Politics, Rutgers, The State University of New Jersey.

[126] Bureau of Labor Statistics, Current Employment Statistics, Table B-5. Employment of women on nonfarm payrolls by industry sector, seasonally adjusted (as of January 8, 2016); and U.S. Government Accountability Office (GAO), "Corporate Boards: Strategies to Address Representation of Women Include Federal Disclosure Requirements" GAO-16-30 (Published December 3, 2015).

[127] Ibid.

[128] Ibid.

[129] Ibid.

[130] Ibid.

[131] Ibid.

[132] Ibid.

[133] Ibid.

[134] Bureau of Labor Statistics, "Highlights of Women's Earnings in 2014" Table 2: Median usual weekly earnings of full-time wage and salary workers, by detailed occupation, 2014 annual averages.

[135] Benjamin Collins and Jody Feder, "Pay Equity: Legislative and Legal Developments" Congressional Research Service (November 22, 2013).

[136] Christianne Corbett, M.A. and Catherine Hill, Ph.D., "Graduating to a Pay Gap: The Earnings of Women and Men One Year after College Graduation" American Association of University Women (October 2012).

[137] Judy Goldberg Dey and Catherine Hill, "Behind the Pay Gap" American Association of University Women (April 2007).

[138] Francine D. Blau and Lawrence M. Kahn, "The Gender Wage Gap: Extent, Trends, and Explanations" (January 2016).

[139] CONSAD Research Corporation, "An Analysis of the Reasons for the Disparity in Wages Between Men and Women" (January 12, 2009).

[140] World Economic Forum, "The Global Gender Gap Report 2015" (November 2015).

[141] Organisation for Economic Co-operation and Development (OECD), "Key charts on employment: gender wage gap" (accessed March 18, 2016); Francine D. Blau and Lawrence M. Kahn, "The Gender Pay Gap" NBER Reporter, National Bureau of Economic Research (Summer 2001); and Francine D. Blau and Lawrence M. Kahn, "The Gender Pay Gap: Have Women Gone as Far as They Can?" Academy of Management Perspectives, vol. 21, no. 1 (2007) pp. 7-23.

[142] Laura Addati, Naomi Cassirer and Katherine Gilchrist, "Maternity and paternity at work: Law and practice across the world" International Labour Organization (2014).

[143] Ibid.

[144] Swedish Institute, "10 Things That Make Sweden Family-Friendly" (accessed January 20, 2016).

[145] OECD, "Closing the Gender Gap: Act Now" (December 17, 2012), pp. 171.

[146] For additional discussion see Gretchen Livingston, "The link between parental leave and the gender pay gap" Pew Research Center (December 20, 2013).

[147] Andrew Lord, "8 Countries That Put U.S. Paternity Leave to Shame" Huffpost Business (June 17, 2015).

[148] OECD, "Closing the Gender Gap: Act Now" (December 17, 2012), pp. 203.

[149] OECD, "Closing the Gender Gap: Act Now" (December 17, 2012), pp. 209.

[150] World Policy Center, Global Map: Are workers entitled to sick leave from the first day of illness? (accessed January 20, 2016). According to the World Policy Center, other countries that do not guarantee paid sick leave include Angola, Guinea-Bissau, India, Laos, Liberia, the Republic of Korea, Mozambique, Nepal, Somalia and Sierra Leone.

[151] National Partnership for Women & Families, "Paid Sick Days Statutes - Updated March 2016" (accessed March 11, 2016). This includes cities within states that have already enacted a statewide paid sick leave law. It also includes San Diego and Pittsburgh, where implementation of the passed paid sick leave legislation is currently on hold.

[152] Ibid.

[153] National Partnership for Women & Families, "Paid Sick Days: Low Cost, High Reward for Workers, Employers and Communities (November 2015).

[154] Bureau of Labor Statistics, "Employee Benefits in the United States – March 2015" Table 6. Selected paid leave benefits: Access, National Compensation Survey, March 2015 (July 24, 2015).

[155] Ibid.

[156] Bureau of Labor Statistics, "Employee Benefits in the United States – March 2015" Table 6. Selected paid leave benefits: Access, National Compensation Survey. March 2015 (July 24, 2015).

[157] Elise Gould and Tanyell Cooke, "High quality child care is out of reach for working families" Economic Policy Institute (October 6, 2015).

[158] OECD, Family Database: PF3.1 Public spending on childcare and early education (2011) (accessed January 6, 2016).

[159] OECD, Family Database: PF3.4 Childcare support, Chart PF3.4.B (accessed January 20, 2016).

[160] European Observatory of Working Life, Press Release "Government announces family policy reforms" (June 24, 2003).

[161] GOV.UK Press Release "Government brings forward plans to double free childcare for working families" (June 1, 2015).

[162] Ariane Hegewisch and Janet C. Gornick, "Statutory Routes to Workplace Flexibility in Cross-National Perspective" IWPR (2008); and Council of Economic Advisers, "Work-Life Balance and the Economics of Workplace Flexibility" (June 2014).

[163] Claudia Goldin, "A Grand Gender Convergence: Its Last Chapter" *American Economic Review*, vol. 104, no. 4 (2014) pp. 1091-1119.

[164] Ibid.

[165] John Jankowski, "Caregiver Credits in France, Germany, and Sweden: Lessons for the United States" *Social Security Bulletin*, vol. 71, no. 4 (2011) pp. 61-76.

[166] Ibid.

[167] Heidi Hartmann, Ph.D , "Enhancing Social Security for Women and other Vulnerable Americans: What the Experts Say" IWPR (July 2014).

[168] European Commission, "Tackling the gender pay gap in the European Union" (2014).

[169] Department of Education and Government Equalities Office "Mandatory Gender Pay Gap Reporting - Government Consultation on Draft Regulations" (accessed March 16, 2016).

[170] U.S. EEOC, "Press Release: EEOC Announces Proposed Data to Annual EEO-1 Reports" (January 29, 2016).

[171] U.S. EEOC, "FY 2012 Congressional Budget Justification" (February 2011), pp.14.

[172] National Women's Law Center, "Fact Sheet: How the Paycheck Fairness Act Will Strengthen the Equal Pay Act" (May 2015).

[173] American Association of University Women, "The Simple Truth about the Gender Pay Gap, Spring 2016 Edition" (February 6, 2016), p. 19; and IWPR, "Pay Secrecy and Wage Discrimination" (January 2014).

[174] United Nations Entity for Gender Equality and the Empowerment of Women, "Constitutional Database" (accessed January 19, 2016).

[175] For more information see "The Equal Rights Amendment – 111th Congress" Office of Congresswoman Carolyn B. Maloney (July 13, 2009).

[176] Thomas H. Neale, "The Proposed Equal Rights Amendment: Contemporary Ratification Issues" Congressional Research Service (April 8, 2014).

[177] Ibid.

[178] "Frequently Asked Questions" The Equal Rights Amendment Website (a project of the Alice Paul Institute in collaboration with the ERA Task Force of the National Council of Women's Organizations), accessed January 20, 2016.

[179] Ibid.

[180] According to BLS, collection of data on median usual weekly and hourly earnings began in 1979. While there was some collection of earnings data prior to that (not regular collections), they are not comparable to this series because different questions were used. The Census Bureau publishes women's median annual earnings as a share of men's median annual earnings going back to 1960. (See Historical Income Tables Table P-40 Women's Earnings as a Percentage of Men's Earnings by Race and Hispanic Origin).

[181] As defined by the U.S. Census Bureau, a full-time, year-round worker is one who worked full time (at least 35 hours per week) for 50 or more weeks during the preceding calendar year.

[182] National Women's Law Center, "Fact Sheet: FAQ about the Wage Gap" (September 2015).

[183] Bureau of Labor Statistics, "Highlights of Women's Earnings in 2014" Table 1: Median usual weekly earnings of full-time wage and salary workers, by selected characteristics, 2014 annual averages (November 2015).

[184] Bureau of Labor Statistics, "Highlights of Women's Earnings in 2014" Table 8: Median hourly earnings of wage and salary workers paid hourly rates, by selected characteristics, 2014 annual averages (November 2015).

[185] Pamela Coukos, "Myth Busting the Pay Gap" U.S. Department of Labor Blog (June 7, 2012).